Strategic Organizational Devel

Strategic Organizational Development & Change

Compiled and Edited by:

Jonathan H. Westover, Ph.D.
Utah Valley University

First printed/published in 2014 in the USA
by HCI Press
as part of Leading Innovative Organizations series

Library of Congress Cataloging-in-Publication Data

Strategic Organizational Development and Change / Jonathan H.
Westover, editor.
        p. cm. -- (Leading Innovative Organizations series)
ISBN-13: 978-0692326282 ; ISBN-10: 0692326286 (HCI Press)

1. Organizational Development. 2. Organizational Change. 3.
Organizational Strategy. I. Westover, Jonathan H.

Table of Contents

Strategic Organizational Development and Change

About the Editor

Dr. Jonathan H. Westover is an Associate Professor of Management and Associate Director of the Center for the Study of Ethics at Utah Valley University, specializing in international human resource management, organizational development, and community-engaged experiential learning. He is also a human resource development and performance management consultant. Already a recipient of numerous research, teaching, and service awards and fellowships early in his academic career, Jonathan also recently was named a Fulbright Scholar and was visiting faculty in the MBA program at Belarusian State University (Minsk, Belarus), and he is also a regular visiting faculty member in other graduate business programs in the U.S., UK, France, Poland, and China. Prior to his doctoral studies in the Sociology of Work and Organizations, Comparative International Sociology, and International Political Economy (University of Utah), he received his B.S. in Sociology (Research and Analysis emphasis, Business Management minor, Korean minor) and MPA (emphasis in Human Resource Management) from the Marriott School of Management at Brigham Young University. He also received graduate certificates in demography and higher education teaching during his time at the University of Utah. His ongoing research examines issues of globalization, labor transformation, work quality characteristics, and the determinants of job satisfaction cross-nationally.

Acknowledgements

This text was compiled, edited, and adapted from open source texts at http://www.saylor.org/books and created under a Creative Commons Attribution-NonCommercial ShareAlike 3.0 License without attribution as requested by the work's original creator or licensee. Please contact me for a free copy of the e-text. I would like to thank the many anonymous individuals who contributed their own wisdom and writing to this edited work, particularly those who contributed to the text *Focusing on Organizational Change*. Most of all, I would like to publically thank my wife (Jacque) and my six wonderful children (Sara, Amber, Lia, Kaylie, David, and Brayden) for all of their love and support!

Preface

We live in an increasingly hyper-competitive global marketplace, where firms are fighting to stay lean and flexible in an effort to satisfy increasingly diverse and specialized consumer demand around the world. Additionally, with the shifting global economy in recent decades and the emergence of the technology and service-oriented knowledge organizations, how do organizations effectively drive positive change? How do organizations effectively foster a continuous learning and innovation culture, better motivate employees, and make sound organizational decisions? What can organizational leaders do to promote ongoing organizational agility that will have a measurable impact on increased firm effectiveness and employee productivity? How can organizations more successfully manage organizational knowledge to achieve strategic organizational goals and add value to all organizational stakeholders? These are just some of the pressing questions facing the organizations of today.

Strategic Organizational Development and Change is a text that provides a comprehensive introduction to a broad range of organizational change topics and explores the wide sweeping impacts for the modern workplace, presenting a wide range of cross-disciplinary research and business cases in an organized, clear, and accessible manner. Additionally, unlike other organizational development and change texts, this book has a strong strategic management and practitioner focus. It will be informative to management students, academics and instructors, while also instructing organizational managers, leaders, and human resource development professionals of all types seeking to understand proven practices and methods to creating organizational systems and culture to promote ongoing organizational learning and innovation to drive firm effectiveness in an increasingly competitive global economy.

Chapter 1

The Strategic Leader's New Mandate

The ability to hold two competing thoughts in one's mind and still be able to function is the mark of a superior mind.
 - F. Scott Fitzgerald

The meeting of two personalities is like the contact of two chemical substances: if there is any reaction, both are transformed.
 - Carl Jung

Strategic leaders [1] today are facing unrelenting pressures to deliver results. Indeed, whole books are being written based on the central premise that the purpose of leadership is to deliver results—on time and within budget. [2] In light of these withering pressures to deliver predictable short-term results, most leaders conclude that their only option is to react quickly to problems and opportunities as they arise and forget about long-term thinking.

This pressure to change is real and increasing. Ed Lawler and Chris Worley note,

> *An analysis of the Fortune 1000 corporations shows that between 1973 and 1983, 35 percent of the companies in the top twenty were new. The number of new companies increases to 45 percent when the comparison is between 1983 and 1993. It increases even further, to 60 percent, when the comparison is between 1993 and 2003. Any bets as to where it will be between 2003 and 2013?* [3]

[1] I distinguish between "strategic leaders" in this book who are in senior leadership positions at the strategic apex of the organization, and other "leaders" who can demonstrate leadership separate and distinct from their authority or position within the organization.
[2] Ulrich, Zenger, & Smallwood (1999).
[3] Lawler and Worley (2006), p. 1.

1.1 The New Mandate for Change Leadership

While executive leaders must react quickly to current problems and opportunities, they must also look to and prepare for the future. And while only a skilled few will have the ability to be "visionary," one thing you know that the organization will need to do is to become more agile, flexible, and nimble. In other words, their long-term mandate is to build organizational capacity for change.

In the best-selling book titled *The Seven Habits of Highly Successful People*, Stephen Covey argued that all individuals must invest time and energy in balancing "production" with "production capacity." Furthermore, Covey boldly states that "every production problem is a production capacity opportunity." [1] While this insight was directed to individuals and personal effectiveness, it also applies to strategic leaders and collective effectiveness.

One popular approach to making the organization more open to change is to resort to fear-based tactics in order to heighten the sense of urgency and productivity of the entire organization. For example, "burning platforms" is a popular phrase for many change programs—a metaphor for the notion that time is running out and we will all burn up and die if we don't act immediately to move to or create an entirely new platform or organization.

In the short term, fear works. And in some cases, a fear-based "burning platform" is the most appropriate way to get the organization to quickly understand the need to change and to respond in new ways. By way of a painful recent illustration, Chief Electronics Technician Mike Williams really did have to jump 100 feet off the burning oil rig owned and operated by British Petroleum in the Gulf of Mexico on April 20, 2010, in order to live—he had to jump or else get consumed by the lethal flames, smoke, or explosions—it was literally a matter of life or death. [2]

However, invoking the burning platform metaphor too often or for too long a period of time will lead to unhealthy "burnout" for the change champions, create Dilbert-like cynicism from middle managers, and lead to pathological resistance from frontline workers. In short, organizational change is painful, but if there is too much pain or the pain lasts for too long a period of time, the organization begins to break down. [3]

Consequently, the new leadership mandate for the 21st century is delivering results in the short term while building change capacity for the long term. Capacity-building change initiatives take time, and short-term productivity sometimes suffers when the organization explores new organizational values, norms, systems, and routines. Capacity building requires trial, experimentation, and learning and these activities are not efficient in the short term. In general, learning is rarely efficient, but it is essential for organizations to be effective.

Michael Beer and Nitin Nohria, both organizational scholars at the Harvard Business School, argue for a more balanced perspective of leadership as well. Essentially, they assert that the two leading theories of organization are "Theory E," where the firm pursues short-term results in order to elevate the enterprise, and "Theory O," where the firm seeks to build long-term organizational capacity. [4] Since much more is known about "Theory E" than "Theory O" approaches, this book will focus on the much newer and harder-to-execute theory.

Consequently, strategic leaders today need to be ambidextrous in their approach to leadership. This balancing act is much more challenging than pushing hard for short-term results or nurturing the organization so that new ideas and capabilities emerge in the long term. Because current pressures usually shove long-term objectives to the side, leaders are proving to be much more practiced in reacting to putting out brush fires in today's organizations than in preparing the organization to be more change capable. Nonetheless, leaders must learn to fly the plane while rewiring it in flight [5]—this is the mandate of the 21st century.

[1] Covey (1989), p. 202.   [4] Beer and Nohria (2000).
[2] Pelley (2010).   [5] Judge and Blocker (2008).
[3] Abrahamson (2000).

1.2 Leadership Mandates in Context

The notion of the ambidextrous leadership mandate is clear and compelling in principle, but in practice it can be quite challenging. First, individuals tend to be better at one skill than another. For example, leaders who thrive on generating short-term tangible results are often not as adept in building long-term organizational capabilities (and vice versa). Just as right-handed persons struggle with left-handed lay-ups in basketball, leaders often display a "handedness" in their leadership orientation. Of course, with awareness and practice, ambidexterity can be developed, but this is not a trivial endeavor. Hopefully, this book will offer compelling logic and some ideas as to how this ambidexterity can be cultivated.

A second complication is that sometimes the official leadership mandate is different from the unofficial one within a particular organization. When the official mandate does not align with the unofficial one, it can be devastating to leaders and organizations. Laurence Stybel and Maryanne Peabody are organizational consultants based in the Boston area. They coined the term "stealth mandate" and observed that it is very common for an executive to be given one leadership mandate while others in that same organization are operating with a completely different mandate.

> *Generally speaking, leadership mandates fall into one of three major categories: continuity, good to great, and turnaround. Continuity means business as usual: carrying on policies, procedures, and strategies. A typical example is the interim CEO, selected to maintain the status quo until a permanent CEO is found. Good to great refers to Jim Collins's bestselling book of the same name. A good-to-great mandate is essentially this: We've been doing fine, but we can—and need to—do even better. Turnaround means dramatic changes are necessary: No business process, job, or strategy is sacred.* [1]

For example, CEOs are sometimes hired to move the organization from "good" to "great." However, if the top management team or the board of directors or both are operating with a "continuity" mandate, the unofficial mandate clashes with the official one, and chaos often unfolds. When the official mandate is fundamentally different from the unofficial mandate, steps must be taken to bring them into alignment. Usually, this requires extraordinary conflict management skills and emotional maturity on the part of the leader.

A third complication that can challenge this ambidextrous approach to leadership is when the environmental context doesn't allow the executive sufficient discretion to pursue short-term results while building organizational capacity for change. Some industries are in terminal decline, and the executive leader is not afforded the "luxury" of working for long-term survival. Some nations put employment ahead of productivity, and the executive leader is not allowed to challenge underperforming units. And some organizational cultures value stasis over excellence. All these constraints can conspire to limit executive discretion so that change capacity is not developed.

Fourth, and perhaps most importantly, organizations are built to perform within an established order, not to change. Managers are often rewarded for predictable results so organizational bureaucracy often gravitates to exploitation over experimentation, efficiency over effectiveness, and leveraging previous learning over generating new insights. Hence, it is a rare organization that is "built to change." [2]

[1] Stybel and Peabody (2006), p. 11.
[2] Lawler and Worley (2006).

1.3 The Leader's Pursuit of Multiple Objectives

In the fast-paced world that we live in with all its distractions, some might argue that it isn't possible to pursue multiple objectives.

Essentially, this is the logic behind pursuing shareholder value above all else. Indeed, there is some evidence to support this notion as some leaders pursue the stakeholder approach in order to avoid accountability, preserve self-interested behavior, or both. For example, a fascinating recent study found that the firms that were rated highest in corporate social responsibility were also the ones most likely to engage in earnings management—essentially using accounting tricks to deceive those outside of the firm. [1]

However, even "Neutron Jack" (Welch) understood that a myopic focus on shareholder value would threaten the very survival of General Electric. As such, even while he was laying off thousands of workers and shedding dozens of business units, he was working behind the scenes to build GE's organizational change capacity, which emerged as his official focus in his later years as CEO. Which leads to a very important insight—the public objective or objectives announced to the rest of the organization do not have to be the same as the private objective or objectives pursued by the leaders of the organization. [2]

Louis Gerstner, the former CEO and Chairman of IBM who engineered a historic turnaround at that iconic firm, writes that leaders must be focused and they must be superb at executing a strategy. [3] For Gerstner, focus generated short-term results while execution was about building organizational capacity for change—both efforts were required to return IBM to its industry-leading role.

In summary, the leader's mandate of the 21st century is to "avoid the tyranny of 'or' and pursue the genius of the 'and.'" [4] Those who are entrusted with authority within an organization must pursue results *and* build organizational capacity for change (OCC). This book details just what organizational capacity for change is, and provides guidance as to how that capacity can be developed. I have been studying this capacity for over 10 years now and have developed a reliable and valid inventory for measuring OCC. With that inventory, I have amassed a considerable amount of data that has been helpful to other executive leaders as they seek to develop their firm's OCC. This book helps to explain exactly what OCC is and to provide insights as to how executive leaders can pursue it.

[1] Prior, Surroca, & Prior (2008).   [3] Gerstner (2002).
[2] Welch and Welch (2005).   [4] Collins and Porras (1994).

1.4 Mapping the Chapters of This Book

This book seeks to assist leaders in building their organizational capacity for change. It is written for any executive who seeks to be more proactive toward change, and wants the process to be less painful and somewhat more predictable. In this first chapter, my objective is to challenge the conventional views about leadership and change.

Chapter 2 "What Is Organizational Capacity for Change?" begins by examining what is organizational capacity for change, and why it is important. The one thing that you can be certain of in your future is that you and your organization will need to change. This chapter explores how some organizations do that well. In addition, you will learn that organizational capacity for change comprises eight dimensions, as summarized in Figure 1.1 "Eight Dimensions of Organizational Capacity for Change", and that each succeeding chapter goes into depth on each of these dimensions.

Figure 1.1 Eight Dimensions of Organizational Capacity for Change

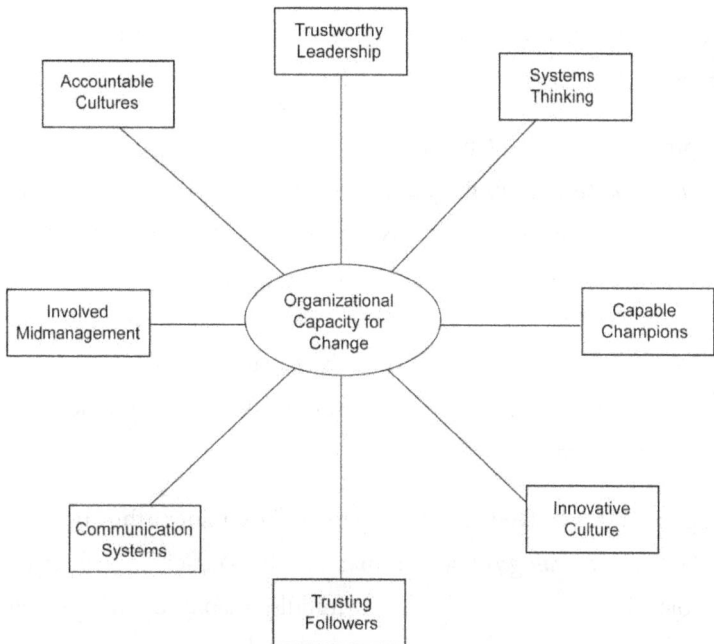

The first dimension of organizational capacity for change, *trustworthy leadership*, is the focus of Chapter 3 "Trustworthy Leadership". This chapter explains that authority is not enough to make an organization change capable; the strategic leaders must be perceived to be competent and looking out for the well-being of the rest of the employees in the organization. However, a strategic leader or leaders behaving in a trustworthy fashion are not enough; the followers within the organization must be favorably disposed to trusting their organization. In essence, you also need *trusting followers* to be change capable. Therefore, in Chapter 4 "Trusting Followers", we examine how important effective followership is within an organization in order to make it change capable. Together, these two human capital dimensions combine to yield the level of organizational trust that exists within the organization and throughout the organizational hierarchy.

Chapter 5 "Capable Champions" explores the important role of *capable champions* within change-capable organizations. Change champions are those individuals within the senior executive group, the middle management ranks, or both who drive the change initiatives within an organization. These individuals are often mavericks and they don't normally fit in well in bureaucratic structures. However, their misfit nature is exactly what is needed in order to drive change successfully.

Chapter 6 "Involved Midmanagement" examines the role that *involved middle managers* play in making the organizational change capable. In many organizations, middle management has been hollowed out, downsized, and replaced by computers. The remaining middle management group is often uninvolved with the strategy formation design initiatives. This is a mistake. Middle managers have a unique and important role to play in enhancing the change capability of the organization. When an organization comprises capable champions and involved midmanagement, then you have an opportunity for lateral leadership and effective influence without authority—a key ingredient for making your organization more agile.

Chapter 7 "Systems Thinking" focuses on *systems thinking* within the organization. Organizations are complex living systems that are not properly understood by linear thinking and analysis. In this chapter, we explore how systems thinking gets cultivated so that organizational learning is accelerated. Then in Chapter 8 "Communication Systems", the importance of effective *communication systems* is investigated. When an organization combines systems thinking with high-functioning communication systems, systemic knowledge is created and dispersed throughout the organization.

The final two chapters explore the role of organizational culture and change. Specifically, Chapter 9 "Accountable Culture" demonstrates the importance of having an *accountable culture* where there are consequences for employees that fail or succeed. However, this cultural attribute needs to be counterbalanced with an *innovative culture*, which is the focus of Chapter 10 "Innovative Culture". Together, these two dimensions of organizational change capacity—accountability and innovativeness—help to ensure that the organization efficiently marshals scarce resources while creatively looking to the future.

Chapter 11 "The Big Picture" provides a "big picture" perspective on organizational capacity for change, as well as guidance for assessing your organization's capacity for change. Specifically, it provides ideas and suggestions for utilizing the survey listed in "Appendix A: Organizational Capacity for Change Survey Instrument" to collect data and the benchmark data listed in "Appendix B: 8 Dimensions and Factor Loadings for Organizational Capacity for Change", "Appendix C: Organizational Capacity for Change Benchmarking", and "Appendix D: Organizational Capacity for Change Benchmarking" that can be used for comparisons between your organization and other organizations that have already been assessed. Finally, "Appendix

E: Additional Resources" contains some simulations and readings that can be used to further explore the organizational capacity for change framework and contains additional resources for teaching, researching, and learning about organizational capacity for change.

Chapter 2

What Is Organizational Capacity for Change?

It is not the strongest of the species that will survive, nor the most intelligent, but the one most responsive to change.

  - Charles Darwin

The only person who likes change is a wet baby.

  - Price Pritchett

If the leader's new mandate is to prepare for change in the future while delivering results in the present, then what specific preparation is required? My central thesis is that the strategic leader's preparation for the future entails building organizations' capacity for change, and that is the focus of the remainder of this book. In other words, this book is about helping executives fulfill the strategic leader's new mandate. [1]

The business press is filled with many recent and ongoing stories of organizations that failed to adapt and change to an increasingly fluid and unpredictable environment. Indeed, a widely cited statistic is that "more than 70% of all organizational change initiatives fail." [2] Nonetheless, one of the arguments why senior executives are worthy of the lofty compensation packages that they currently command is based on the widely-held view that effective leaders and change agents are rare, but essential to cope with the volatile and hypercompetitive environments that many organizations find themselves in today. [3]

In response to this pressure to change, scholars and consultants are increasingly focusing on the nature and dynamics of organizational change in an effort to distill lessons learned from previous successes and failures, and provide guidance to change agents to improve their future success rate. Notably, in a recent online search of articles written on "organizational change" in the last 20 years, I discovered that there were more than 25,000 articles published in a prominent online search engine named Proquest. [4] This suggests to me that the topic is of great importance to those seeking to change organizations, but that much that is written about organizational change by organizational scholars is not improving our success rate. In sum, there is more to be learned about this important subject and this book attempts to fill that gap.

[1] Bossidy and Charan (2002).   [3] Kaplan (2008), p. 5.
[2] Higgs and Rowland (2005), p. 121.   [4] ProQuest Research Library (2010).

2.1 Primary Reasons for Failure to Bring About Change

I believe that there are three primary reasons for our poor track record in changing organizations. One of the primary reasons for the failure of both scholars and practitioners to successfully develop and utilize a comprehensive yet parsimonious approach to organizational change is our collective failure to understand the systemic nature of change. Too often, organizational members operate in "departmental silos" that focus on local optimization at the expense of the entire system. Furthermore, the senior executives in charge of the overall organizational system (as well as the academics who study them) often fail to understand the interdisciplinary nature of their organizations as they are trapped in the myopia of their own backgrounds or disciplinary blinders.

Organizations are complex, interdependent social entities with relationships operating both within its boundaries and outside of its boundaries. Too many practitioners, in their "bias for action," focus on a single dimension of organizational life or a single lever of organizational change. Change agents need to be reflective, as well as capable of influencing others. Organizational leaders need to be comprised of confident but humble CEOs and by well-functioning top management teams who collectively understand the entire organization, not a lone wolf with a reputation for individualism and boldness.

A second reason why so many change initiatives fail is that organizational change takes time, and time is one of the most precious commodities in the 21st century. In a recent article written by myself and a former doctoral student, we argued that organizations no longer have the luxury to go offline while the new information system is being built, the foreign venture is being launched, or the new technology is being analyzed. As such, change agents must "rewire" the plane while it is flying if the organization hopes to survive and perhaps prosper in the future. [1] Clearly, this is no easy task when everyone around you is arguing for you to "hurry up"!

A third reason why so many change initiatives fail is that our conception of what makes us human is overly mechanistic, narrow, and limited. Our traditional view of organizations is that they are hierarchies with power concentrated at the top with rational and logical employees operating throughout this hierarchy. While it is true that all organizations are hierarchical in some form and that organizational members are rational at times, this viewpoint is limited and not terribly realistic.

Organizational change is not only a rational activity but also an emotional one that challenges deep-seated human fears and inspires human hope. Indeed, John Kotter recently argued that change is predominantly about matters of the heart, not the head. [2] Organizations can operate in mechanical ways, but they also comprise living human beings who want meaningful work that allows them to "have a life" outside of work. As such, by assuming that all organizational change is rational and logical in nature where fear, political positioning, and turf wars rage, one wonders why any change initiative might work.

[1] Judge and Blocker (2008), p. 915.   [2] Kotter and Cohen (2002).

2.2 The Typical Reaction to Challenging Environmental Pressures

In my executive education classes and consulting projects, I ask my students and clients what their planning horizon is since strategic leaders are responsible for the long-term performance of their organizations. One response by the president of a major nonprofit medical center is instructive: "Ten years ago, my planning horizon was 5 years into the future. Five years ago, it was 2 years. In today's environment, where health care reform is the flavor of the day, it is now down to 2 months." Another CEO of a Fortune 500 chemicals company told me, "There is merciless pressure to deliver the financial results that Wall Street expects each and every quarter.

Even though Wall Street denies this, our stock price often gets punished by looking beyond the next 3 months."

Both of these quotations from CEOs, one from the nonprofit sector and the other from the for-profit sector, imply that the best that senior executives can do is to respond quickly to an increasingly volatile and demanding environment. While I agree that organizations today must be more "nimble" in reacting to such things as unexpected competitor moves, a seemingly short-term focus by the owners of the organization, and unpredictable "disruptive" technologies [1] that change the competitive dynamics of an industry overnight, this focus is overly narrow and too reactive. To succeed in the 21st century, organizations today must not only nimbly and flexibly respond to their changing environments but also build capacity for change.

---

[1] Christensen (1997).

2.3 Organizational Capacity for Change Defined

Organizational capacity for change (OCC) can be conceptualized as the overall capability of an organization to either effectively prepare for or respond to an increasingly unpredictable and volatile environmental context. This overall capability is multidimensional, and it comprises three ingredients: (a) human skill sets and resources, (b) formal systems and procedures, and (c) organizational culture, values, and norms. As such, OCC is *a dynamic, multidimensional capability that enables an organization to upgrade or revise existing organizational competencies, while cultivating new competencies that enable the organization to survive and prosper.*

Peter Vaill argued that organizations increasingly operate in "white water" where executives have only partial control, yet effective navigation of a boat on the rapids requires everyone in the boat to react efficiently and effectively to the white water all around them. [1] While I like this metaphor, I would add that the navigator must also prepare the boat and the rest of the team for the oncoming white water.

Robert Thames and Douglas Webster use a different metaphor to describe the context in which firms operate today, namely—a hurricane or an earthquake. They state,

> *To many organizations, change comes like a hurricane season. Everyone knows it's coming. It is the same every year. The only thing we don't know is "Who will it hit this time?"…To other organizations change comes like the earthquake. We may never see it coming but have this nagging feeling that it is.* [2]

Whether your industry or national economy seems like white water rapids, an oncoming hurricane, or a potential earthquake, organizations must prepare in advance, not just react when the "environmental jolt" is experienced. That advance preparation is what I am calling organizational capacity for change. Organizations with relatively high change capacity can successfully shoot the rapids, weather the hurricane, or continue operating during and after a devastating earthquake. Organizations with relatively low change capacity are at the mercy of their environment and much more subject to luck and chance.

I have been researching the nature of organizational capacity for change in hundreds of organizations in a wide variety of industries for over 10 years. In previous research I have found that the higher the aggregate organizational capacity for change is, the higher the subsequent environmental [3] and financial performance. [4] In other words, organizational capacity for change is positively correlated with, and is likely to lead to, superior financial and environmental performance.

In addition, I have also found that the importance of organizational capacity for change increases with the volatility of environmental uncertainty. In other words, common sense and systematic empirical research show that the more your environment is changing, or is about to change, the more important your organizational capacity for change is.

Finally, after reading literally hundreds of articles and dozens of books on organizational change, I have been able to distill the concept of organizational capacity to change down to eight separate and distinct dimensions. [5] These dimensions are briefly described in the sections that follow, but they will be more extensively discussed in later chapters.

[1] Vaill (1991), p. 2.
[2] Thames and Webster (2009), pp. 11–12.
[3] Judge and Elenkov (2005).
[4] Judge, Naoumova, Douglas, & Koutzevol (2009).
[5] Judge and Douglas (2009).

2.4 The Eight Dimensions of Organizational Capacity for Change

Trustworthy leaders. No lasting, productive change within an organization ever happens without a modicum of trust between its members. As a consequence, the first essential dimension for OCC is the extent to which an organization is perceived to be led by trustworthy leaders. A trustworthy leader is someone who is not only perceived to be competent in leading the organization but also perceived as someone who has the best interests of the organization as their priority. This is why Jim Collins found that organizations that were changing for the better tended to be led by senior executives who were perceived to be humble servants of the organization, but were also passionate about ensuring a bright future for the organization. [1]Organizational change is risky. In order for employees to change their perceptions and behaviors, they have to trust their leaders. As such, a proven record of trustworthiness on the part of the leaders is essential to bring about experimentation with a new order of things.

Trusting followers. Leaders are only half of the equation when it comes to organizational change; the other half is the followers. I once worked with an executive at Alcoa who was perhaps one of the most trustworthy executives I ever met. He was honest to a fault, a first-rate engineer, who worked his way up through the executive ranks to a prominent leadership position. He had a deep and sound understanding as to where his business unit needed to change, but he had a problem—his plant was highly unionized and it had a long history of management missteps and labor union outrage. Interestingly, the union leaders did trust this particular plant manager, but they didn't expect him to stay there long and they did expect corporate headquarters to replace him with someone who was not trustworthy. As a result, this business unit had a leader who was perceived to be trustworthy, but the ubiquitous lack of trust on the part of the rest of the organization prevented any major change initiative from progressing.

Psychologists tell us that all individuals have a "disposition to trust" others. [2]This disposition is influenced by such things as a person's genetic background, family norms, and work-related experiences. When an organization is filled with a critical mass of individuals who are hopeful, optimistic, and trusting, it will be well positioned to experiment with new ways of operating. When an organization is dominated with a critical mass of individuals who are cynical, pessimistic, and not trusting, it will not be well positioned to engage with organizational change initiatives. In sum, a second key dimension of organizational capacity for change is the overall level of trust held by the employees of the organization.

Capable champions. Individuals, and hence organizations, tend to be inertial. In other words, change takes extra energy and it is much easier to keep doing things the way in which we are accustomed to. Consequently, organizations must identify, develop, and retain a cadre of capable change champions in order to lead the change initiative(s). Within small organizations, these champions are often the same as the head of the organization. Within medium and larger organizations, these champions are often drawn from the ranks of middle management.

Rosabeth Moss Kanter first identified this new breed of managers and she called them "change masters." She defined change masters as "those people...adept at the art of anticipating the need for, and of leading, productive change." [3]Professor Kanter's central thesis is that if an organization is to change and innovate, power needs to be focused on or delegated to certain talented and energetic individuals, or both.

These "corporate entrepreneurs" are experts in building formal and informal coalitions to makes changes and get things done within an established organization. They know how to directly and indirectly handle political opposition. They often lead a group of "mavericks" and "bend the rules" in order to bypass bureaucratic obstacles. They are often very goal directed and know how to deliver on their promises. In sum, these change champions are often "sponsored" by top management to spearhead change initiatives. If an organization does not have capable champions, change initiatives often stall.

Involved middle management. Middle managers are those who link top executives to frontline workers. Department heads are classic examples of middle managers, but there are many other types of linkages. While it is undeniable that today's organizations are flatter hierarchies with fewer middle managers than in the past, their role in helping to bring about change is still important. While change champions often come from the middle management ranks, middle managers can passively or actively block change initiatives due to their unique position within an organization.

Steven Floyd and Bill Wooldridge were among the first scholars to note the importance of middle managers when focusing on strategy formation and organization change. As they point out,

The capability-based model of competition puts managerial knowledge at the forefront of competitive advantage. The knowledge of middle managers may become crucial in recognizing an organization's shortcomings and in broadening its capacity for change [italics added]. Perhaps even more important, the middle manager's centrality in the information network creates the potential for them to become a driving force in organizational learning. Realizing this potential, however, demands a new set of management expectations. [4]

Whenever any new organizational change initiative is announced, one of the first things that employees consider is "how will this affect me?" While every organization is going to have doubters and naysayers, one of the keys to enhancing organizational change capacity is to get a critical mass of the organization excited about the potential change. Middle managers are pivotal figures in shaping the organization's response to potential change initiatives, so their involvement is crucial to organizational capacity for change.

Systems thinking. Organizational change capacity involves more than just the "getting the right people on the bus and the wrong people off the bus," however. It also depends on a proper organization infrastructure. One of the key infrastructure issues that influence or retard an organizational change initiative is what is called "systems thinking." These are the rules, structural arrangements, and budgetary procedures that facilitate or hinder an organization-wide—as opposed to a "segmentalist"—approach to organizational change. While segmentalism works quite well for routine procedures, it is anathema to the study of nonroutine events such as strategic decision making, organizational change, or both. [5]

Peter Senge is a seminal author in this area. In his classic 1990 text, titled *The Fifth Discipline*, Senge wrote about how systems thinking can enhance an organization's ability to experiment, adapt, and learn new ways of operating. [6]Systems thinking, according to Senge, focuses on how the individual being studied interacts with the other constituents of the system. Rather than focusing on the individual's or organizational units within an organization, it prefers to look at a larger number of interactions within the organization and in between organizations as a whole. In sum, an organizational infrastructure that promotes systems thinking is another key dimension of organizational change capacity.

Communication systems. A second infrastructure dimension, and one that complements the systems thinking dimension, is what is called "communication systems." This dimension involves such things as e-mail networks, face-to-face meetings, telephone calls, and corporate announcements all being focused on the conveyance of the value for and the means for implementing a proposed organizational change. Organizational change requires reflection and action. Too often, there is a gap between thinking and doing. [7] Consequently, many observers of failed and successful organizational change initiatives emphasize the importance of communication in order to convert knowledge into action.

For example, John Kotter argues that almost every change leader fails to accurately estimate the frequency, range, and amount of communication required to bring about change. [8] Malcolm Gladwell argues that in order for organizations to "tip" in a new direction, convincing and persuasive communication is essential. [9] And Ed Lawler and Chris Worley argue that effective formal and informal communication systems are essential to the creation of organizations that are "built for change." [10] In sum, effectively designed and delivered two-way information about the change initiative is essential to building organizational capacity for change.

Accountable culture. A fourth and final infrastructure dimension is the degree to which an organization holds its members accountable for results. In my observation, most organizations generally excel on this dimension. However, when the organizational culture gets focused on innovation, accountability often gets ignored. While individuals need autonomy in today's organizations to pursue innovative new ideas, they also need to be held accountable for delivering results on time and within budget. At the very least, they need to explain the failure to honor deadlines, resource constraints, or both.

Another term for an "accountable" culture is a "results-based" culture. [11]Accountable cultures do not focus on how the work is done, but they do help to carefully monitor the outcomes of results produced. As a result, accountable cultures track whether a deadline was reached or whether the activities were executed under budget or not, and seek to discern what teams and individuals hindered or facilitated successful change. Of course, change is inherently unpredictable so there must be some executive judgment involved with the evaluation of results. However, fostering innovation and change does not mean that innovators and change agents are given a blank check with no deadlines. In sum, organizational capacity for change is also dependent on effective reward and control systems.

Innovative culture. Tom Peters and Bob Waterman wrote powerfully as to the importance of an organizational culture "in search of excellence" in their classic text on America's best-run companies. [12] Similarly, John Kotter and Jim Heskett demonstrated a powerful correlation between corporate culture changes and subsequent firm performance improvements over 4 to 10 years of time. [13] And Clayton Christensen showed how corporate cultures often work to thwart innovation and change, particularly when the organization is a market leader. [14]

The culture of an organization defines appropriate behavior, and motivates individuals and offers solutions where there is ambiguity. It governs the way a company processes information, its internal relations, and its values. [15] Some organizational cultures value innovation and change, while many others value stability and equilibrium. In sum, an organizational culture that emphasizes the importance of organizational change and innovation is a third infrastructure dimension that is critical to organizational change capacity.

[1] Collins (2001).

[2] Cook (2001).

[3] Kanter (1983), p. 13.

[4] Floyd and Wooldridge (1996), p. 23.

[5] Kanter (1983), pp. 28–35.

[6] Senge (1990).

[7] Pfeffer and Sutton (2000).

[8] Kotter (1996).

[9] Gladwell (2002).

[10] Lawler and Worley (2006).

[11] Ulrich, Zenger, & Smallwood (1999).

[12] Peters and Waterman (1982).

[13] Kotter and Heskett (1992).

[14] Christensen (1997).

[15] Hampden-Turner (1992), p. 11.

2.5 Concluding Thoughts about Organizational Capacity for Change

In response to pressures to deliver short-term results, leaders and organizations often neglect building their capability to be productive. This book provides a description of how to overcome that purely reactive focus so that the organization can survive and prosper over the longer term.

This capability, or organizational capacity for change as I call it, contains eight different dimensions—four of the dimensions focus on critical human capital and four focus on social infrastructure. Many authors have written insightful books and articles about aspects of organizational capacity for change, but few have attempted to synthesize these writings into a coherent whole. Furthermore, this concept has been rigorously developed and researched in the organizational sciences, having undergone peer review of several scientific articles about it.

The remainder of this book elaborates on what the leader's role is in creating organizational capacity for change, focuses on each of its eight dimensions in more depth, and provides practical ideas for diagnosing and enhancing your organizational capacity for change. In each subsequent chapter, I provide a detailed review of each dimension and discuss its relationship to organizational capacity for change. At the end of each chapter, seven actionable suggestions are made to help practitioners enhance this particular dimension of their organization.

Chapter 3

Trustworthy Leadership

The glue that holds all relationships together—including the relationship between the leader and the led—is trust, and trust is based on integrity.
- Brian Tracy

The first responsibility of a leader is to define reality. The last is to say thank you. In between, the leader is a servant.
- Max De Pree

3.1 What Is Trustworthy Leadership?

Trustworthiness can be thought of as the quality of someone being competent and benevolent so that others can safely be in partnership with that person. As Brian Tracy suggests earlier, trustworthiness is important to all human relationships, but it is essential for leadership effectiveness and the ability to prepare for and drive organizational change.

All change requires a partnership between leaders and followers. In any partnership situation, the leader must first demonstrate competence. After all, why should anyone follow the leader if the leader first does not demonstrate skill or competence in envisioning the future, making that vision a reality, or both? Certainly, followers are compliant every day with those in authority, but compliance is largely effective only in stable and unchanging situations. In unstable and changing situations, a trusting disposition among a critical mass of the employees is essential. If the followers' disposition is largely compliant, change will be temporary or nonexistent. Indeed, it is foolish for anyone to follow a leader who is not deemed competent to lead. In other words, it is appropriate for followers to resist change when the leader has not demonstrated competence in leading. [1]

But competence must be coupled with benevolence for one to have sufficient trust in a leader to agree to be led. Competence is a reflection of skill and followers want and need their leaders to be skillful, but what if the leader skillfully takes advantage of his or her followers? This implies that to be skillful or competent as a leader is necessary, but not sufficient grounds for leading change.

The popular press focuses on charisma as the mark of leadership, but history is replete with charismatic leaders who attracted lots of followers and then led them in self-centered and manipulative ways. Thus, the leader must benevolently care for his or her followers' well-being, and they must be convinced that they are being cared for.

A metaphor that I like to use with executives when discussing the importance of benevolence is that of a knife. Knives are tools that can be handled with great skill, such as preparing food for a meal or defending from an attack. However, if the followers turn the knife over to the leader, they first want to be sure that the leader will not use the knife on them. The knife is a metaphor for power, and leadership involves the proper use of power. All knife-wielding leaders need to show that they know how to use a knife, and that they will not use that knife against their followers.

Some argue that those in authority positions within an organizational pyramid are the leaders of the organization, and that all that is needed to lead is for the followers to respect the authority of the position. This conception worked in the past, but works less and less in today's organizations, as I will discuss later in this chapter. Indeed, many observers now argue that we are seeing the decline of authority and rise of trust as an organizing principle. [2] Clearly, to be effective today, strategic leaders need to combine trust with authority. Authority is helpful, but it is not enough to lead others effectively.

[1] Kelley (1992).   [2] Hardy (2007).

3.2 Trustworthy Leadership Yields Trust and Cooperation

Chester Barnard was one of the first writers who observed that trustworthy leadership yields trust and cooperation. Barnard was a rare individual who worked in a major corporation (New Jersey Bell) for 40 years and rose to a position of leadership; afterward, he wrote insightfully about that leadership experience. Barnard noted that the key to organizational survival and prosperity was cooperation, communication, and a shared sense of purpose. He further argued that leaders could only lead when they were perceived to be trustworthy by the rest of the organization. Even in the 1930s, Barnard argued that authority is completely a function of the willingness of subordinates to cooperate with the leader. Barnard was well ahead of his time. [1]

Warren Bennis argues that the traditional idea of a "heroic" individual leading followers through sheer force of will is a myth.

Instead, he argues for creative and productive partnerships among a group of individuals as being the only viable way forward. He emphasizes the importance of those in leadership positions needing to learn how to generate and sustain trust so as to enable organizations to survive the increasingly turbulent changes swirling around and within today's organizations. [2]

Some argue that there is so much distrust in the workplace today that leaders can no longer rely on trustworthy leadership as an organizing principle. While it is true that there is very little trust in most of the organizations today, it is not true that mistrust on the part of followers cannot be diminished over time. For example, in a recent experimental research study, trustworthy players were found to be more effective in obtaining mutual cooperation than untrustworthy players, even given a history of distrust prior to engagement. Trustworthy players did this through signaling reassurance, rather than fearful messages, to the potential partner. [3] In sum, trustworthiness is essential to change, and it can even overcome a mistrusting disposition.

Others argue that it is human nature to resist change, and that organizational changes are even more challenging than individual change. However, this viewpoint is too pessimistic, and both the empirical evidence and common sense suggest that human beings generally want to be part of something that is changing for the better, if there is trustworthy leadership driving that change and if they are involved in helping to decide the nature and pacing of the changes. [4]

Dynamic stability is the new normal; static states of equilibrium are becoming rarer in organizations. Trustworthy leadership helps to reduce the pain associated with organizational change, [5] and it yields increased employee engagement. [6] Trustworthiness can lead to more creative work, and organizational innovation is impossible without trustworthy leadership. [7]

[1] Barnard (1938).

[2] Bennis (1999b).

[3] Kydd (2000).

[4] Peus, Frey, Gerhardt, Fischer, & Traut-Mattausch (2009).

[5] Abrahamson (2000).

[6] Dittmar, Jennings, & Stahl-Wert (2007).

[7] Littlefield (2004).

3.3 Trusting Cooperation Makes All Change Possible

Organizations can function for short periods of time where part or all of the top management team are viewed as untrustworthy. However, this will thwart the organization's overall ability to change, and in the long term all organizations must change in order to survive. When in a crisis situation, however, trusting cooperation, and hence trustworthy leadership, is essential to survival. [1] It is a truism that when the ship is sinking, the captain of the ship must be obeyed in order to save the ship and its crew. If the ship's captain is not viewed as trustworthy, the rational thing for the crew to do is abandon the ship, regardless of what the captain is urging.

Many if not most of today's changes are complex and interrelated. For example, business process improvements typically cross multiple departments and multiple levels of an organization. Previous research has shown that preparing for change and the presence of trust can enable an organization to avoid "silo" thinking and focus on the organization's well-being. [2]

Middle managers are the linkage between top executives and frontline employees. During all change initiatives, middle managers often feel torn between the changes urged by the "tops" against the resistance expressed or observed by frontline workers. Trustworthiness on the part of change agents enables middle managers to maintain the linkage between tops and the frontline, rather than actively or passively resisting the change. [3] In sum, all change requires trusting cooperation, and that is why trustworthy leadership is a critical dimension of organizational capacity for change.

[1] Booher (2002). [3] Weber and Weber (2001).
[2] Hall (2008).

3.4 Trustworthy Leadership Is Valuable and Rare

To secure competitive advantages today, organizations need valuable and rare resources. Previous research has demonstrated that trustworthy leadership is not only valuable; it is also rare. [1] For example, recent research has shown that trustworthy leaders are often able to establish trusting climates within organizations, and that the higher the trust level, the more profitable the organization is. [2] Furthermore, other research has demonstrated that trustworthy leadership speeds up the decision-making process as well as the implementation speed of new strategies. [3] This suggests that trustworthy leadership helps to assure not only the organization's survival but also its future prosperity.

Fortunately or unfortunately, trustworthy leadership is relatively rare within today's organizations. In a recent national poll, it was revealed that 80% of Americans do not trust the executives who lead major corporations. Even worse, roughly half of all managers do not trust the top executives in their own firms. [4] In another national survey, 62% of all workers claim to have no aspirations to any leadership role within their organization because they perceive the leaders to be untrustworthy. [5] Clearly, having a trust gap between consumers and corporations is problematic, but it is even more challenging when middle managers and frontline employees lack trust.

There are many reasons given for the rareness of trustworthy leadership within today's organizations. Clearly, many executives did not act in a trustworthy fashion in the aftermath of the Enron, Worldcom, and AIG scandals. [6] Indeed, some observers even declare that "trust is dead." [7] While I personally do not believe that trust is dead, I do agree that the level of trust that Americans have for their leaders is not very high.

Another reason given for the lack of trust in today's corporate leaders is the view that compensation levels are becoming excessive, and that executive leaders are greedy and self-serving above all else. [8] While many workers have been laid off in recent years, or are assuming increasing duties with no pay increases, executive compensation has been increasing dramatically. Clearly, the perception of injustice and unfairness on the part of executive leadership is not conducive to fostering trust and cooperation among the rest of the organization.

A third common reason why it is getting harder to trust executives is because the shareholder value ethic is eroding the trust of the general public, especially in publicly held corporations. The consulting firm McKinsey notes that building trust among key stakeholders is a strategic concern for any corporation, and that generalized stakeholder trust is a major competitive advantage since it is so rare. [9] In sum, trustworthy leadership is not only valuable; it is also rare. The good news here is that when the strategic leader is viewed as trustworthy, a noteworthy competitive advantage is generated.

[1] Barney and Hansen (1994).
[2] Burton, Laurdisen, & Obel (2004).
[3] Roth (2008).
[4] Hurley (2006).
[5] Harris (2010).

[6] Pellet (2009).
[7] Kempner (2009).
[8] Williamson (2008).
[9] Bonini, Hintz, & Mendonca (2008).

3.5 Trustworthiness Is Becoming Increasingly Important

Notably, leadership trustworthiness is not only rare, but it is also becoming more important. Daniel Yankelovich tracks social trends throughout the United States, and he argues that a new social contract is replacing the old one. Yankelovich asserts that as we transition from an industrial to an information-based economy, the employment relationship is changing dramatically, and that these changes require that organizations be managed and led differently. [1]

There are hints as to where these changes are all leading. Some note that organizations are evolving into federations and networks, and evolving away from pyramids and hierarchies. [2] When an organization is organized more as a network, then "lateral leadership" is more the norm than is vertical leadership. [3] If this assessment is correct, being at the top of the pyramid or hierarchy will be less critical to getting things done in future organizations.

Others note that the millennial generation now outnumbers the baby boom generation in today's workforce. This new generation of workers, having seen their parents get laid off, outsourced, and downsized, is much less loyal to the organization than previous generations. As Marshal Goldsmith observes, this generation wants you to earn their trust; trust is not given automatically. [4]Therefore, as millennials increasingly infiltrate our organizations, organizational leadership is going to have to earn their trust in order to be effective, and that trust is not easily earned.

Another trend in organizational life is the growing pervasiveness of virtual teams that are often spread out in a wide variety of time zones and countries. Since work cannot be directly observed or controlled, accountability systems must focus on outcomes and "control" is exerted through trusting partnerships. [5] In general, the trend for future organizational life is clear: leaders need to rely more on soft power and persuasion than on hard power and control. [6] In sum, trustworthy leadership is not only valuable and rare, but it is also increasingly important.

[1] Yankelovich (2007).

[2] Bennis (1999a).

[3] Kuhl, Schnelle, & Tillman (2005).

[4] Goldsmith (2008).

[5] Henttonen and Blomqvist (2005).

[6] Nancheria (2009).

3.6 Practices for Cultivating Trustworthy Leadership in Your Organization

There is no recipe or formula for building trustworthy leadership within an organization. Human beings are too variable for a recipe and human relationships come in all shapes and sizes. After all, leadership development is an "inside job" that requires character development, and character development was the focus of a previous book of mine. [1] However, there are some behavioral principles for those individuals and organizations seeking to make their organizations more change capable.

Practice 1: Become Skillful in Leading Others

Leadership takes skill and all skills can be developed over time. Without previous experiences in leading others through a change initiative, it is not possible to become a trustworthy leader. [2] Hence, anything that an organization can do to accelerate and enhance the leadership skills of its managers will yield long-term benefits in also enhancing the organization's capacity to change. [3]

However, having a formal leadership development program is not enough to generate skillful leaders. In a recent review of these programs at eight major corporations, the differentiating factor that separated the successful programs from the unsuccessful programs was whether or not personal follow-up was part of the program or not. Personal follow-up involved such things as reminder notes to keep working on the development plan, one-on-one sessions with an executive coach or peer, and sufficient time and resources to work on important attitudes and behaviors unfolding in real time. In other words, leadership development is a contact sport. [4]

Practice 2: Learn How to Speak With and Listen to Associates

One of the problems with much that has been written about leadership and communication is that too much has been focused on telling the rest of the organization what the leader wants to do and helping to persuade the organization that resistance to change is a bad idea. This is only part of what is required. In order to build the leader–follower relationship, time and energy must be invested so that fears, concerns, and doubts can be expressed, alternative viewpoints can be discussed, and challenges to the vision can be articulated.

Most change initiatives fail because they do not consider the emotional aspects associated with change, and trustworthy leadership that communicates well can be an important antidote to counteract that obstacle to change. Indeed, noted author and change guru John Kotter argues that it is important to understand what people are feeling and to speak more directly to their anxieties, confusion, anger, and distrust. [5]

Interestingly, recent research reveals that the more communication that goes on between executives, the more trustworthy the communicators view each other to be. In a study of 50 senior managers within a multinational firm, it was reported that those executives who communicated more often were more likely to view others in the organization as more trustworthy. [6] Perhaps this is why interactive communication forums such as town hall meetings, online blogs, and two-way video sessions are becoming staples of organizational life.

Practice 3: Know Your Values and Act with Integrity

A key element of trustworthiness is consistency over time. The best way to be consistent is to know your values and act in concert with those values. If the leader or leaders are not clear about what their values are and what values they want to emphasize within the organization, they are likely to send out mixed messages to the rest of the organization.

Subordinates pay attention to what leaders say and do. When the message changes, or more importantly, when the message stays the same and the leader's actions are not consistent with that message, trust is destroyed. One of the key factors noted in Ford's recent success as compared to General Motors' and Chrysler's struggles was described as "talking the walk, and walking the talk." [7] In other words, Ford executives were able to build up more trust with their employees than executives at the other Detroit firms. Knowing your values and acting consistently with them is harder to do than one would think, but building trust in the absence of consistency between espoused and enacted values is virtually impossible.

Practice 4: Think "Win-Win" as Much as Possible

If employees are to trust their leaders, they need to know that their leaders genuinely care about them. This doesn't mean that the leader must avoid conflicts and "play nice" all the time. It does mean that employees know that the leaders of the organization are not just in the game for themselves. Pragmatically speaking, leaders must seek win-win options as much as possible and employees need to know that the leader is looking to create a win for them. [8] In other words, followers want to know that you care about them before they are willing to trust you and follow you. [9]

Interestingly, organizations that went from being good to great were all led by relatively humble leaders who were more focused on building the organization than on their own well-being. Humility is not a traditional aspect used to describe effective leaders, but it is consistent with generating the organizational trust necessary to pursue a bold new vision, change initiative, or both. In sum, caring about the well-being of the entire organization and putting its well-being on a par with your own is essential for building organizational change capacity.

Practice 5: Be Authentic and Human; You Don't Have to Be Perfect

Because the building of a trusting relationship takes time, it is not a one-time event. While we live in a society that is very unforgiving of mistakes, in order to build trust within an organization, it is more important to be authentic and human than it is to be perfect. When a mistake is made by a leader, it should be owned and acknowledged. Sometimes that acknowledgment needs to be made public; sometimes it needs to be private. The following quote is instructive in this regard:

Apologies can create the conditions for constructive change. An apology can also serve to strengthen an organization. Apologizing by admitting a mistake—to co-workers, employees, customers, clients, the public at large—tends to gain credibility and generate confidence in one's leadership…To apologize is to comprehend and acknowledge one's error, to act justly; it requires that the truth be told without minimizing or rationalizing the behavior. [10]

Part of authenticity is being candid and transparent. However, leaders should selectively reveal their weaknesses since too much disclosure can be inappropriate in certain times and places. [11] In other words, it is possible to overdo this candor and undermine one's trustworthiness.

Practice 6: Seek Respect, Not Friendship, From Your Subordinates

As this chapter suggests, organizational leaders need to earn the trust and respect of their followers. However, this does not mean that leaders need to be friends with their coworkers. Friendship at work is a wonderful thing, but far more important is the respect that others have for the leadership of the organization.

Respect is earned through being fair and just. And fairness applies to not only what the policy is but also how the policy is implemented. Indeed, recent research found that employee openness to change was even more influenced by how justly the policy was implemented than by how fair the policy was perceived to be in actual substance. [12]

Practice 7: Trust Others a Bit More; Control Them a Little Less

Relationships are reciprocal in nature. There must be give and take for them to work properly. If leaders want the organization to trust them, then they must learn to trust the organization. While this prospect can be terrifying to some leaders with their fixation on control and predictability, it is an essential ingredient to building organizational capacity for change.

I personally had to deal with this issue myself recently. My 12-year-old daughter and a friend of hers and I visited the boardwalk in Virginia Beach where we live. The girls wanted to rent a four-person bicycle and so we did just that. Being the most experienced driver in the group, I assumed the steering role at the front left-hand side of the bicycle. However, after a few minutes, I offered to let my daughter steer the vehicle on the bicycle path. I made that offer with some trepidation knowing that her eye–hand coordination was not very developed and her ability to focus left much to be desired. Furthermore, the bikeway was quite crowded with other bicycles and many pedestrians nearby. However, I wanted her to learn to trust her driving ability and to know that I trusted her, so I made the offer. She readily accepted, and sure enough, the bicycle careened off the bike path into a bush in a few minutes when someone unexpectedly stepped in front. However, I kept my mouth shut and we did it again and she did much better the second time. Notably, my daughter said this was the highlight of our trip to the beach, and she seemed to walk a little taller and prouder after this little experiment.

Of course, the consequences of driving a bicycle off the path are not as bad as driving an organization off the path, so my personal example is rather trivial compared with trusting others to "step up" within an organization. However, the principles are the same and the outcome is illustrative. Overall, having a balance between trust and control is essential for building organizational trust.

[1] Judge (1999).

[2] McCall, Lombardo, & Morrison (1988).

[3] Tichy and Cohen (1997).

[4] Goldsmith and Morgan (2003).

[5] Kotter and Cohen (2002).

[6] Becerra and Gupta (1999).

[7] Drickhamer (2004).

[8] Covey (1989).

[9] Kouzes (2005).

[10] Stamato (2008), p. 1.

[11] Goffee and Jones (2000).

[12] Chawla and Kelloway (2004).

Chapter 4

Trusting Followers

Do not trust all men, but trust men of worth; the former course is silly, the latter a mark of prudence.
 - Democritus

There are people I know who won't hurt me. I call them corpses.
 - Randy Milholland

Trust makes all change possible. Trust refers to a person's belief that others make sincere efforts to uphold commitments and do not take advantage of that person if given the opportunity. [1] As discussed in the previous chapter, trustworthy leadership is an important ingredient to engendering a trusting organizational environment in which change can take place. However, effective leadership is incomplete unless there is effective followership. [2] After all, leadership is a relationship, not a position. If the leader's partners, the followers, are not sufficiently trusting, then organizational change capability will be impaired.

I came to this somewhat counterintuitive realization when working with a talented executive leader at Alcoa. This individual was a very strong and trustworthy leader—he had strong technical and interpersonal skills, had succeeded in every previous managerial role within Alcoa, was confident but humble, and he genuinely cared about his followers. Because of his strong track record and his considerable future potential to join the executive ranks, he was given increasingly difficult managerial positions within the company. When he was made the plant manager of a large but troubled and underperforming plant within the Alcoa system, he realized that the employees were not inclined to trust him or his leadership team. They were unionized, which gave them the power to stand up to management, and had been used and abused for many years. Previous plant leaders had tried all sorts of Machiavellian tactics to break or bend the union into submission. The end result was pervasive mistrust among most employees and within the overall plant. During his 5 years at the plant, the union gradually came to trust him. However, they told him that he would soon be promoted and replaced by "another untrustworthy jerk," which is exactly what happened.

In general, it has been shown that there are three things that interact to build or tear down organizational trust. First, there is the trustworthiness of the leader or change agent. This was our focus in the previous chapter. Second, there is the propensity or disposition to trust those in authority positions. Finally, there is the risk associated with trusting. [3] The second and third determinants of organizational trust are the focus of this chapter.

[1] Child and Rodrigues (2004).
[2] Kelley (1992).

[3] Mayer, Davis, & Schoorman (1995).

4.1 Employees' Collective Propensity to Trust

People differ in their inherent disposition to trust others. "Propensity will influence how much trust one has for a trustee prior to data on that particular party being available. People with different developmental experiences, personality types, and cultural backgrounds vary in their propensity to trust."[1] In other words, it takes emotional intelligence to follow as well as to lead well. [2]

The central issue is whether those who are *not* driving change within an organization see change as an opportunity for growth or a threat to their well-being. There is considerable organizational research that demonstrates that the label of "threat" or "opportunity" is influenced by the perceiver as much as the actual event, if not more so. [3]

Michael Maccoby, an organizational psychologist, helps us to understand why some employees are predisposed to follow the leader and why others are not. Using the Freudian concept of transference, Maccoby argues that transference is the emotional glue that binds people to a leader. When there is positive transference, employees trust their leaders, work hard, and are highly motivated. When there is negative transference, employees distrust their leaders, do just enough to get by, and are not motivated. [4]

In addition to an employee's formative relationships, previous history also influences his or her propensity to trust. As the old saying goes, "Fool me once, shame on you; fool me twice, shame on me." It has been my observation that bad management leads to the creation of unions; and when a union forms, everyone loses— management, employees, customers—everyone.

However, disposition to mistrust is not limited to blue collar laborers. One recent research study of salespersons is particularly telling. A global Fortune 500 firm agreed to partner with the United

Nations philanthropic organizations, and some social scientists were asked to study employees' perceptions associated with this partnership. Interestingly, if the employees perceived top management to be insincere, then the overall organization's social responsibility initiatives were perceived to be "window-dressing" and not worthy of employee support. However, if the employees perceived their executives to be sincere, then the organization's social responsibility initiatives were perceived to be "positive" and worthy of support. [5] The key takeaway here is that the same overall corporate initiative was viewed differently according to the employees' perception of executives' sincerity.

4.2 Risk Associated With Trusting Others

Some proposed changes are relatively riskless, so it is relatively costless for employees to go along with a change initiative. However, many changes proposed by change agents carry relatively high costs for employees, and therefore it is rational for employees to be more cautious. In sum, when risk is evaluated to be "reasonable." the employee is inclined to trust the change agent and "buy in." [1]

But the perceived riskiness of a current change proposal is not the only element that influences the risks associated with trusting the change agent. Another issue is the weight of history. Organizational trust evolves over time. Some have observed that it is slow to build and quick to be destroyed, as evidenced by the quick demise of Enron. [2]

Another issue that is looming larger and larger for organizations is the rise of flextime, outsourcing, and virtual organizations. It has been observed that these efficiency-creating administrative realities of the 21st century make organizational trust more fragile since face-to-face interactions are a much more robust way to build and maintain trust. [3] In other words, temporal and spatial distance between employees and their leaders makes trust that much more important, but also more fragile and risky.

[1] Das and Tend (2004).   [3] Ramo (2004).
[2] Currall and Epstein (2003).

4.3 Benefits of Pervasive Organizational Trust

When an organization has employees who are generally trusting of senior executives, then organizational trust is high. Previous research has shown a relationship between organizational trust and organizational learning, [1] hope, [2] and organizational innovation and change. [3] Effective followership requires the proper organizational context as well as effective and trustworthy leadership.

As discussed previously, organizational trust is fragile and can be destroyed relatively easily. However, motivated followers can be a source of competitive advantage, and trusting followers is fundamental to becoming a change-capable organization. Furthermore, it is becoming more valuable over time. Organizational trust provides an anchor and some stability when everything else is changing. Having some predictability and psychological safety when everything is in flux and changing is a valuable resource. [4]

And there is some good news about organizational trust within the context of the larger environment. Previous research has shown that it is possible to build organizational trust in low-trust societal contexts. For example, one study found that some of the highest performing firms in post-Soviet Lithuania in the 1990s were those where organizational trust was relatively high. [5] Similarly, the J. Walter Thompson advertising agency survived and even prospered in the 1930s during the Great Depression in the United States due, in part, to the relatively high levels of organizational trust within that same organization. [6]

---

[1] Jones (2001).
[2] Ozag (2001).
[3] Jelinek and Bean (2010).
[4] Grey and Garsten (2001).

[5] Pucetaite, Lämsä, & Novelskaite (2010).
[6] Mishra (2009).

4.4 Practices for Building the Trusting Followers Dimension

If you are interested in building organizational trust in order to make your organization or organizational unit more change capable, the following are some actionable ideas that you can pursue to make that a reality.

Practice 1: Know What the Propensity to Trust is Within Your Organization

It is important for executives to systematically collect data on the state of the overall organization, particularly with respect to organizational trust. After all, what gets measured gets managed. The easiest way to do this is through anonymous surveys of employees. However, it can also be done by watching for mistrust signals, such as employee sentiment that a new policy was unfair, or the firing of a manager was a mistake, or the launching of a new project was ill-considered. While there is no substitute for executive intuition, trust data can add precision and clarity to the situation. In a later chapter, we provide guidance as to how that data might be reliably collected and analyzed. Trend information is particularly important since comparisons over time tend to be the best indicator of how the current top management team is affecting organizational trust. Of course, knowledge and understanding of previous organizational events that damaged or encouraged trust is valuable information.

Practice 2: Dialogue With Employees; Don't Just Talk to Them

People trust others who they believe understand them. [1] How does an old-line manufacturer in a stagnant industry manage to grow 25% per year for 10 years? The answer, made in a recent *Inc. Magazine* cover story, is, by taking its employees seriously and listening to them. Atlas Container makes cardboard boxes. They also practice "open book management" and engage in workplace democracy. [2] In another instance, the Ford Motor Company turned its poorest-performing plant operating near Atlanta to one of its best, simply by engaging in dialogue with the entire 2,000-member unit. [3] Both of these anecdotes illustrate that a tremendous amount of employee trust and energy is liberated simply by engaging in dialogue, rather than in the more traditional top-down communiqués that occur throughout the business world.

Practice 3: Encourage Constructive Dissent from Subordinates

Robert Kelley argues passionately that leaders need constructive dissent from their subordinates in order to lead effectively. Clearly, this needs to be done with tact and diplomacy, but it can be done. Notably, the Intel Corporation trains each and all of its technically skilled employees in conflict management, and even goes so far as to identify its ability to surface and resolve conflict in the workplace as a distinctive competency. [4] As such, the creation of an environment where constructive dissent is the norm is a valuable and rare organizational attribute.

Engaging in constructive dissent takes courage and willingness to incur the wrath of the rest of the organization. In general, organizations do not react well to those who disrupt the social harmony. [5] Consequently, training and education as to how to respectfully disagree with a supervisor can be helpful. However, nothing replaces the importance of demonstrated examples. For example, when human resource directors constructively disagree with CEOs, their advice and contributions are taken more seriously. [6] In sum, constructive dissent is essential if you want to create trusting partnerships with your followers.

Practice 4: Be Fair and Consistent in Applying Corporate Policies

Inconsistencies and unfairness erode organizational trust very quickly. Individuals who vacillate, easily change their viewpoint depending on whom they are talking with, or refuse to make a decision because it may upset some people erode trusting partnerships. [7] While top executives are constantly confronted with exceptional circumstances and a continually changing environment, they must take care to avoid showing favoritism to one individual or group to the exclusion of other individuals or groups. Once again, this is easier said than done. What do you do when your star salesperson cuts corners with expense accounts? How fairly is affirmative action handled in your corporation? How do you handle requests by legitimately hurting subordinates who ask for exemptions from standard operating procedures? Sometimes, the manner in which these issues are handled are just as important as what is decided. In any event, follower trust is not possible in a work environment that is not generally seen to be fair and consistent.

Practice 5: Design Reward Systems to Support Trusting Partnerships

Most reward systems are focused on individual contributions, but collaboration and trust do not thrive in such a system. Rewards and accountability are important, and they earn a dedicated chapter in this book later on. However, their impact on organizational change capacity has a special power when it comes to engendering trust in the organization. Having said that, changing reward systems is very difficult to do. Simply recognize that it is a sheer waste of time to reward A (i.e., individual competition) while hoping for B (i.e., collaborative partnerships), as the classic article by Steven Kerr attests. [8]

Practice 6: Remove Employees Who Repeatedly Destroy Trust

As Jim Collins suggests, you need to "get people off the bus who don't want to go where you are going." [9] While creating trust is typically a "warm and squishy" idea, there is a hard side to trust that involves punishment and sanctions applied to those who are just not capable of creating trusting relationships, nor are they inclined to do so. The following is an excerpt by Jim Collins that explains why this is so important:

> *When it comes to getting started, good-to-great leaders understand three simple truths. First, if you begin with "who," you can more easily adapt to a fast-changing world. If people get on your bus because of where they think it's going, you'll be in trouble when you get 10 miles down the road and discover that you need to change direction because the world has changed. But if people board the bus principally because of all the other great people on the bus, you'll be much faster and smarter in responding to changing conditions. Second, if you have the right people on your bus, you don't need to worry about motivating them. The right people are self-motivated: Nothing beats being part of a team that is expected to produce great results. And third, if you have the wrong people on the bus, nothing else matters. You may be headed in the right direction, but you still won't achieve greatness. Great vision with mediocre people still produces mediocre results. [10]*

Exceptional people build trust; mediocre people destroy trust. Avoid hiring and get rid of those who destroy trust in your organization. As Jack and Suzy Welch succinctly stated, "Send the jerks packing." [11]

Practice 7: Talk Straight and Be Transparent

There is considerable pressure on leaders to waffle and evade or just not be accessible. The belief is that the rest of the organization just does not understand the complexities and nuances of the information held at the senior-most level. There is a grain of truth to this belief; however, leaders need to understand that straight talk is essential for creating organizational trust. Recent research demonstrates that positive transparency on the part of leaders can greatly enhance followers' trust disposition. [12]

Interestingly, Microsoft Corporation has a relatively high level of organizational trust. For example, 9 out of 10 employees at Microsoft Netherlands said they could "ask management any reasonable questions and get a straight answer." This is particularly noteworthy since the organizational unit recently underwent a downsizing experience. [13] The same can be said for labor unions, which is not easy to do in this day of declining union strength. Clearly, straight talk and transparency are keys to enhancing organizational trust in all parts of the organization.

In summary, organizational trust is essential to be change capable. This requires both trustworthy leaders and trusting followers.

[1] Brownell (2000).

[2] Case (2005).

[3] Bunker and Alban (1997).

[4] Thomas (2010).

[5] Mercer (2010).

[6] Stern (2009).

[7] Brownell (2000), p. 11.

[8] Kerr (1975).

[9] Collins (2001b).

[10] Collins (2001b), p. 42.

[11] Welch and Welch, 2006.

[12] Norman, Avolio, & Luthans, (2010).

[13] Maitland (2008), p. 2.

Chapter 5

Capable Champions

Nothing great was ever achieved without enthusiasm.
- Ralph Waldo Emerson

To be a great champion you must believe you are the best. If you're not, pretend you are.
- Muhammad Ali

Top executives increasingly create cross-functional task forces comprised of respected middle managers to serve as a guiding coalition for major change initiatives. However, even when the top management team personally leads a change initiative, such as in life-or-death turnaround situations, individual change champions within the middle management ranks must "step up" if the change is to be successful. Consequently, the "vertical" chain of command, addressed in the previous two chapters (the hierarchical leader–follower relationship), is not enough to create a change-capable organization. Because organizations are removing layers of bureaucracy and because we are moving from an industrial economy to an information-based economy, "lateral" relationships and leadership are becoming more important. This chapter examines one essential part of that lateral relationship, namely, "capable champions."

A capable champion is a middle manager who is able to influence others in the organization to adopt a proposed change without the formal authority to do so. In a systematic study of change champions conducted by McKinsey and Company, they found that these middle managers are different from the typical manager. While traditional managers always seek to make their numbers; change champions seek to satisfy customers and coworkers. Traditional managers hold others accountable; change champions hold everyone accountable, including themselves. In addition, traditional managers are fearful of failure; change champions are not afraid of failure and understand that they have career options outside of this job. In sum, traditional managers analyze, leverage, optimize, delegate, organize, and control with the basic mind-set that "I know best." In contrast, change champions' basic mind-set is to do it, fix it, change it, and that no one person knows best. [1]

Clearly, organizations need to be both managed well and led effectively if they are to be successful over time. However, most organizations are overmanaged and underled, [2] and capable change champions are one of the best antidotes to this organizational imbalance. As Rosabeth Moss Kanter states,

Senior executives can come up with the most brilliant strategy in history, but if the people who design products, talk to customers, and oversee operations don't foster innovation in their own realms, none of that brilliance will make a whit of difference. [3]

[1] Katzenbach (1996).   [3] Kanter (2004), p. 150.
[2] Bennis and Nanus (1997).

5.1 Influence without Authority

Because organization-wide change and innovation frequently goes beyond existing organizational subunits and lines of authority, change champions often need to go beyond their existing authority in order to get things changed. To do this, they need power, which can be thought of as the capacity to mobilize resources and people to get things done. And just as absolute power corrupts, absolute powerlessness on the part of change champions also corrupts in the sense that those who are more interested in turf protection than in the overall organization are not challenged to think and behave in a bigger fashion. [1]

The advantage the change champions bring to the table is their deep knowledge of how things actually are and how things need to change to make the change vision a reality; the disadvantage that they have is their inadequate power base to influence those with whom they have no authority. Consequently, organizations that are "built to change" hire, retain, and promote change champions in sufficient numbers to counterbalance the equilibrium-seeking rest of the organization. In short, change champions are masters of influencing others without the authority to do so.

The first people change champions need to influence is their superiors and the top management team. Not all middle managers know how to "manage up," but this talent is essential. There is a phenomenon operating to varying extents in all organizations known as "CEO disease." This organizational malady is the information vacuum around a senior leader that gets created when people, including his or her inner circle, withhold important information. This leaves the senior leader out of touch and out of tune with the rest of the organization, its environment, or both. [2]

Change champions are adept at selling strategic issues for senior managers to address. Change champions are also courageous enough to challenge senior executives when they are off track or misinformed. And change champions obtain the "sponsorship" of executives to act on the executives' behalf. All of these behaviors require sophisticated political skills and the character to do this well.

In addition to influencing senior executives, change champions must also influence other middle managers to consider and adopt organizational changes. In this case, informal networks of influence must be created or expanded in order to bring about change, neutralize resistance to change initiatives, or both. One of the key ways that change champions do this is by the creation of alliances through exchanges of currencies.

Allan Cohen and David Bradford have written the seminal book on influence without authority, which is the ability to lead others when you do not have authority over them. These authors argue that many different currencies circulate within organizations, and that money is just one of those currencies. Those non-authority-related currencies include such things as inspiration-related currencies (e.g., vision, moral, or ethical correctness), task-related currencies (e.g., the pledge of new resources, organizational support, or information), relationship-related currencies (e.g., understanding, acceptance, or inclusion), and personal-related currencies (e.g., gratitude, comfort, or enhancement of self-concept). [3]

In particular, they emphasize the role of negotiations in creating win-win intraorganizational alliances and partnerships. To do so, they argue that you as a change champion must (a) know and communicate what your goals and intentions are to your potential ally, (b) understand your potential ally's world and what his or her goals and intentions are, and (c) make win-win exchanges that prevent organizational changes from proceeding. [4]

Finally, change champions must influence frontline workers who are not under their direct supervision if the organization is to become change capable. Whenever change initiatives are launched, there are multiple "narratives" that flow through the organization because communication from the "top" is almost always inadequate, and listening from the "bottom" is often filtered. Change champions help to make sense of those often conflicting narratives so that frontline workers feel less threatened by the changes. [5]

Similar to other middle managers, change champions, in order to get changes adopted, can also trade currencies with frontline workers over whom they have no authority. Since frontline workers often feel oppressed and ignored within many hierarchical organizations, the softer skills—such as expressing sincere gratitude, including frontline workers in the change process, and understanding and accepting them—are particularly important to change champions if these alliances are to be maintained.

[1] Kanter (2004), p. 153.
[2] Arond-Thomas (2009).
[3] Cohen and Bradford (2005).
[4] Cohen and Bradford (2005).
[5] Balogun and Johnson (2004).

5.2 Getting Things Done When Not in Charge

Geoffrey Bellman is an organizational development consultant who has written a national best seller about being a change champion. In his book, he says that in order to work effectively with other people over whom you have no authority, it is important to start out by being clear about what you want. Specifically, he states, "Clarity about your vision of what you want increases the likelihood you will reach for it." [1]

He adds that "when we are not doing what we want to do, we are doing what others want us to do." [2] In essence, he argues for the power of an authentic life over the power of organizationally backed authority. One of the implications of such a posture is that becoming a change champion within an organization requires that you be prepared to leave it when or if your life's purpose cannot be pursued. Bellman states it well: "Worse that losing a job is keeping a job in which you are not respected, or not listened to, or not consulted, or not influential, or...you name it, it is your fear." [3]

Similar to other observers, Bellman argues that by keeping the combined interests of yourself and others in mind, you will get things done when not in charge. However, he further adds that many changes and change visions must wait for the proper time to act. In other words, change champions must be politically astute in their timing of change initiatives as they consider the evolving interests of others along with the evolving interests of themselves.

[1] Bellman (2001), p. 118.   [3] Bellman (2001), pp. 110–111.
[2] Bellman (2001), p. 21.

5.3 Rising Importance of Change Champions

Ori Brafman and Rod Beckstrom used a creative analogy from the animal kingdom to illustrate the rising importance of change champions within organizations. They argued that future organizations will function more like starfish, and less like spiders. They state,

> *If you chop off a spider's head, it dies. If you take out the corporate headquarters, chances are you'll kill the spider organization...Starfish don't have a head to chop off. Its central body isn't even in charge. In fact, the major organs are replicated through each and every arm. If you cut the starfish in half, you'll be in for a surprise: the animal won't die, and pretty soon you'll have two starfish to deal with.* [1]

Illustrating their point, they argue that the organizations of the 21st century, what they call "starfish" organizations, are demonstrated by customer-enabled Internet firms such as eBay, Skype, Kazaa, Craigslist, and Wikipedia; "leaderless" nonprofit organizations like Alcoholics Anonymous and the Young Presidents Organization; and highly decentralized religious movements like the Quakers and al Qaeda.

With respect to this chapter, their insights about champions are particularly interesting. A champion is someone who is consumed with an idea and has the talent to rally others behind that idea. Brafman and Beckstrom argue that the passion and enthusiasm of champions attracts followers, and their persistence enables the group to endure all the obstacles to change. Classic champions of the past include Thomas Clarkson, a Quaker driven to end slavery, and Leor Jacobi, a vegan driven to end meat-eating. In the end, this book argues that change champions are as much if not more important to the future survival of the organization than even the formal leaders of the organization.

---

[1] Brafman and Beckstrom (2006), p. 35.

5.4 Practices for Cultivating Capable Champions

To conclude this chapter, I once gain offer seven practices that can enable an organization to cultivate capable champions. As Ralph Waldo Emerson was quoted at the beginning of this chapter, nothing great ever gets accomplished without enthusiasm. Champions are passionate enthusiasts leading change initiatives.

Practice 1: Hire, Develop, and Retain Change Agents

Many senior executives confine themselves to looking only one level down from the top and conclude incorrectly that there are not enough people to lead change initiatives. As a result, they often hire newcomers or consultants too quickly and put them in influential change agent positions. While this is sometimes unavoidable, this approach has a major downside to it since it signals that the senior leadership does not trust existing managers to champion change.

A much better approach is to hire potential change agents to help ensure the organization's future. However, change agents are mavericks by nature, and the hiring decision either consciously or unconsciously screens out individuals "who don't fit in." This is why hiring decisions are often better made by those who have actually led others to be superior to staff persons with no actual leadership experience or background.

Practice 2: Listen to Middle Managers, Especially Those Who Deal Directly With Customers

In the previous chapter, it was emphasized that senior leaders need to dialogue with and listen to their employees. This is especially true of change agents within the middle management ranks. For example, an organizational study of governmental agencies found that senior leaders of agencies that engaged in dialogue with the middle management ranks were much more successful in pursuing change than senior leaders of agencies that used a more top-down, one-way communication style. Change agents have unique and detailed perspectives on the entire organization as well as its customers. Senior leaders need two-way communication to tap this knowledge.

Practice 3: Identify Who Your Change Champions Are

Unusually effective middle managers are tremendous repositories of change champions. A recent *Harvard Business Review* article offers insights on how to identify who the change champions might be. [1] First, look for early volunteers. These individuals often have the confidence and enthusiasm to tackle the risky and ambiguous nature of change. They often feel constrained in their current duties, and are eager for more responsibility. Give it to them.

Second, look for positive critics. Change-resistant managers constantly find reasons why a change proposal won't work, and they seldom, if ever, offer a counterproposal. In contrast, positive critics challenge existing proposals, suggest alternatives, and provide evidence to support their argument. Positive critics offer constructive criticism and positive criticism is essential to being a change champion.

Third, look for people with informal power. They are often middle managers whose advice and help are highly sought after by people all around them. They often have excellent reputations and a lot of "social capital." They typically operate at the center of large informal networks, and know how to work with that network successfully.

Fourth, look for individuals who are versatile. Change champions need to be comfortable with change, and they often adapt more easily to previous organization change more readily and easily than others in the organization. Those who have endured in their career shifts, relocations, or both are more likely to be comfortable with change than those who have not undergone these professional changes.

Finally, look for emotional intelligence in your middle management ranks. Individuals who are aware of their own emotions and those of others, and actively take steps to manage their feelings, are more likely to adapt to an envisioned change. Emotional intelligence is much more important than traditional logical-mathematical intelligence. Using the vernacular of the day, change champions need "emotional" bandwidth. [2]

Practice 4: Recognize and Reward Effective Change Champions

Organizations are designed to reduce variation; change champions are oriented to creating variation. How can these two different orientations co-exist? Clearly, there needs to be a balance here. Unfortunately, most organizations only reward managers who reduce variation and punish or, more likely, ignore those who amplify variation.

Due to the messiness and uncertainty behind change, change champions are more likely to make mistakes. Organizations need to learn to find a way to reward effectiveness in addition to efficiency. Making mistakes is not efficient, but it can be effective. Does your organization recognize and reward an efficiently run organizational unit that hasn't changed much in years as well as an organizational unit that has changed completely, but in the process angered some individuals along the way? Change champions make mistakes, but they learn from their mistakes and they ultimately succeed. As hard as it is for organizations, they need to be recognized and rewarded for doing so.

Practice 5: Train and Develop Middle Managers to Be Change Agents

Noel Tichy argues that effective companies build leaders at every level, and they do this by creating a "leadership engine." This is especially true for the development of change champions. In Tichy's view, the best leaders are "enablers" rather than "doers." They work their initiatives through other people rather than doing it all themselves. They can only accomplish this, he adds, if they develop people sufficiently to ensure that proper execution can occur at all levels. [3]

In large organizations, a formal leadership development program is often created to identify and accelerate the development of change champions. In medium- and small-sized organizations, an informal leadership development program is often sufficient. Regardless of the formality of the program, the key notion here is the importance of "contextualized" training and development. Traditional training and development leads to new knowledge, but has little impact on organizational change. Training and development that is applied to actual work situations through such practices as action learning projects, leadership mentoring, and applied learning endeavors go hand-in-hand with organizational change. [4]

Practice 6: Use Cross-Functional Teams to Bring About Change

Organization-wide change requires cross-function teams to guide the change initiative. Without a cross-functional team, unrepresented organizational units are more likely to resist the change since it is assumed that their voice is not heard or considered. Ideally, the cross-functional team will comprise respected change champions from the various subunits. At a minimum, the team must be led by a change champion.

Cross-functional teams are different from the more traditional functional team. They can speed new product development cycles, increase creative problem solving, serve as a forum for organizational learning, and be a single point of contact for key stakeholder groups. Because of this unique structure and mandate, team leadership is different for a cross-functional team than for a functional team. Specifically, technical skills are relatively less important for these types of teams, but conceptual and interpersonal skills are more important. Hence, the creation and composition of cross-functional teams can be an excellent way to identify and develop your change champions. [5]

Practice 7: Understand the Nature and Power of "Sponsorship"

The sponsor of a change typically comes from the CEO or top management team. Senior leaders authorize change efforts and often provide tangible resources to make that change a reality. However, they also provide intangible and symbolic resources to change champions. If the sponsor announces a change initiative, creates a guiding coalition, and then disappears from view, the organization will notice and the change initiative will suffer. If the sponsor announces a change initiative, creates a guiding coalition, makes him or herself available to support and learn about progress to the team, and regularly voice support for the change initiative, then the change initiative has a much better chance of success.

The relationship between the senior leader and the change champion is particularly important. Since the change champion lacks the authority to get things done and some changes can only be brought about by formal authority, the sponsor must use his or her authority at times to keep up the change momentum. By the same token, change champions should never undertake leadership of a change initiative without solid support and sponsorship by senior leader(s). Without effective sponsorship, change champions are highly unlikely to succeed.

In sum, lateral relationships and influence without authority are as important to organizational change capacity as vertical relationships and authority are. This chapter discusses how creating a cadre of capable champions is essential for bringing about change.

[1] Huy (2001).

[2] Davis (1997).

[3] Tichy and Cohen (1997).

[4] McCall, Lombardo, & Morrison (1988).

[5] Parker (2002).

Chapter 6

Involved Midmanagement

There is an enormous number of managers who have retired on the job.
- Peter Drucker

The Trojans lost the war because they fell for a really dumb trick. Hey, there's a gigantic wooden horse outside and all the Greeks have left. Let's bring it inside! Not a formula for long-term survival. Now if they had formed a task force to study the Trojan Horse and report back to a committee, everyone wouldn't have been massacred. Who says middle management is useless?
- Adam Engst

6.1 The Evolving World of Middle Management

In the 1990s, many firms eliminated midmanagement positions and replaced them with computers. [1] One of the most common terms for this was "delayering," which is standard code for "eliminating all the nonproductive employees in the middle management ranks." The result of all this turbulence is a very different role for middle managers in the 21st century as compared to the 20th century. Midmanagers now have more autonomy relative to the past, but experience much more monitoring. They have more job stress and are working longer hours. And there is less career progression within one firm, but more job hopping between firms. [2]

Meanwhile, there is a "war for talent" going on in the global economy. As such, there is intense and increasing competition for the top 10% of all MBAs and junior managers. As some have observed,

> *The unfortunate mathematical fact is that only 10 percent of the people are going to be in the top 10 percent. So, companies have a choice. They can all chase the same supposed talent. Or, they can do something even more useful and much more difficult to copy—build an organization that helps make it possible for regular folks to perform as if they were in the top 10 percent.* [3]

While these trends and situations vary throughout the world, the overarching trend is for middle managers to be less secure in their jobs and less loyal to their employer. [4] While middle managers have always been torn and conflicted due to their key position in the organizational hierarchy, these feelings are particularly acute today. [5] One of the ways of coping with this new reality is to avoid taking risks and making mistakes, or becoming more passive and less proactive. Perhaps this is why senior managers frequently perceive middle managers as one of the biggest obstacles to change in their organizations. [6] As a result, middle managers are often not involved and engaged with the organization, or its substantive strategic reorientations. This clearly is problematic if the organization seeks to become change capable.

---

[1] Stewart (1995).
[2] McCann, Morris, & Hassard (2008).
[3] O'Reilly and Pfeffer (2000).
[4] Hallier and Lyon (1996).
[5] Hallier and James (1997).
[6] Buchen (2005).

6.2 Middle Managers Contributions to Change

Middle managers have many opportunities to improve the overall change capability of the organization beyond championing strategic initiatives, which was discussed in the previous chapter. Systematic research suggests that middle managers not sponsored as change agents can take initiative on their own to sell ideas, make sense of the proposed changes, and provide essential stability during tumultuous change events. The end result is that "unsponsored" middle managers synthesize and accelerate information flow, facilitate adaptability, and are crucial implementers of deliberate changes. [1]

Selling ideas. In addition to the change agent(s), the senior manager(s), or both, "ordinary" or "unsponsored" middle managers must also sell change if the organization is to be change capable. The traditional selling of ideas is done from the middle manager to his or her subordinates and frontline employees, or "downward selling." In most organizations, a major change initiative is announced by senior managers using lofty but vague visions and slogans. Unfortunately, the typical response of frontline employees is often hostility and fear. Rumors and disaster scenarios rush in to fill the gap. These negative reactions can only be challenged in private meetings between departmental managers after the formal announcement of a proposed change. If the middle manager can translate what the change initiative means to the unit as well as dispel myths and rumors, the organization becomes more change capable. If the middle managers are not sufficiently involved in the change design and objectives, however, this translation does not occur. [2]

In addition to selling downward, middle managers also sell ideas upward to their senior managers. Organizational change begins with the focusing of organization attention, and not all focusing must come from the top of the organization. Indeed, middle managers with their direct contact with customers and unique perspective within the middle of the hierarchy are well positioned for this activity. As recent research has shown, middle managers make formal presentations to top managers as well as bundle new ideas with established strategic goals or issues. [3]

Finally, middle managers also sell ideas laterally. Organizational change typically cuts across multiple organizational units, departments, divisions, or all three. To bring about that change, middle managers across different units must collaborate and work together, without the formal authority to do so. Consequently, the ability to sell ideas laterally and negotiate influence across organizational units is a key contribution by middle managers. [4] In sum, middle managers can be essential salespersons for change initiatives for all those that they come in contact with. Senior executives and change champions are not the only ones to sell the change.

Making sense of change initiatives. Sometimes middle managers are called upon not to "sell" a proposed change, but just "make sense" of it. Organizational life can be confusing and hard to understand, and the emotional nature of change initiatives makes it that much more confusing and "senseless," as Dilbert cartoons repeatedly remind us. Due to their integral role within organizations and the lofty perches of senior managers, middle managers can interpret messages and signals given by top executives to the rest of the organization, and this role can literally be the key factor that unlocks its potential so as to avoid unintended consequences. Indeed, this sense-making function on the part of middle managers has been shown to positively influence restructuring initiatives or an existing operation, [5] as well as the postacquisition integration process of merged operations. [6]

When middle managers are sidelined or blocked from being involved, they themselves can't make sense of the change. This is true even in those instances when the middle managers have blind faith and trust in their senior leaders. Thus, it is harder if not impossible for them to make sense of proposed changes to others. Furthermore, even if they see the wisdom, logic, or both behind a change proposal, they will be less inclined to help others see the wisdom behind it if they have been uninvolved in the design and execution of a particular change.

Providing stability. As discussed previously, any successful change must preserve the core of the organization while changing its periphery. This stabilizing role is best handled by middle managers who are intimately linked with the rest of the organization. Sometimes, middle managers oppose ill-considered changes that violate the organization's core values and norms. As such, not all resistance to change is bad, and middle managers can passively or actively preserve stability through resistance efforts.

However, even when the change initiatives are appropriate and well timed, middle managers can provide a stabilizing influence on the rest of the organization by directly addressing others' fears and simply by listening. Indeed, there is even research to suggest that an essential skill set of middle managers is to act somewhat like an organizational therapist who pays attention to change recipients' emotions and provides healthy perspectives in response to highly emotional reactions. As such, middle managers can provide an "emotional balancing" between organizational continuity and radical changes, and this balancing effect has a short-term and long-term impact on the organization's health and survival. [7]

[1] Floyd and Wooldridge (1996).
[2] Larkin and Larkin (1996).
[3] Dutton, Ashford, O'Neill, & Lawrence (2001).
[4] Cohen and Bradford (2005).
[5] Balogun and Johnson (2004).
[6] Nordblom (2006).
[7] Huy (2002).

6.3 Middle Manager Change Roles

New research suggests that middle managers are often missing in action when radical change is being pursued. However, when they are properly involved and engaged with the change initiative, the change process goes more smoothly and the outcomes are more positive. Four separate roles have been identified by researchers that middle managers fulfill in successful change initiatives, and each is discussed in the following paragraphs.

Entrepreneur. Middle managers are often more diverse than the senior executives are, and this diversity can be a source of creativity and entrepreneurship. A recent *Harvard Business Review* article describes this role well:

> *Middle managers are close to day-to-day operations, customers, and frontline employees—closer than senior managers are—so they know better than anyone where the problems are. But they are also far enough away from frontline work that they can see the big picture, which allows them to see new possibilities, both for solving problems and for encouraging growth.* [1]

So while middle managers are often viewed by senior executives as bureaucrats who constantly obstruct change, they actually are well positioned to be a source of creative entrepreneurial work, especially when it comes to bringing about change.

Communicator. Successful change requires information-rich transmission, such as face-to-face dialogue and observation of body language when discussing the change. Senior leaders simply don't have the time or the energy to communicate one-on-one with employees or in small groups. However, this is what middle managers do on almost a daily basis. When they are properly involved and engaged with the change process (even as change recipients), communication can be improved and clarified, particularly by relying on established formal and informal networks of influence. "As they tap into their networks, middle managers use keen translation skills to communicate change initiatives throughout a work group or a company." [2]

Therapist. Middle managers do a host of things to make the workplace psychologically threatening or safe for an established organization. When the organization confronts change, strong emotions are stirred within employees, which can depress morale, trigger anxiety, and lead to distraction, absenteeism, turnover, depression, workplace violence, and other organizational maladies. If the middle manager is psychologically skilled and aware, many of these painful outcomes can be avoided or minimized during change initiatives. "Middle managers shoulder additional burdens during a period of profound change. Besides the already challenging daily tasks of operations and revenue generation, they provide far more hand holding, practical problem solving, and support than they usually do." [3] Clearly, if middle managers are involved and engaged with the change process, they are more likely to be able to fulfill this role.

Tightrope artist. Middle managers enable the organization to keep producing in the short term, while the organization positions itself for the future. They can slow down the change process when it becomes overwhelming to their unit, and they can speed it up when progress is too slow. They can obtain extra resources for their unit when necessary, and they can trim resources that are being wasted. They can support those in their unit who understand the purpose of the change but need personal support, and they can challenge those who fight the change due to self-interested behavior. In sum, successful organizational change requires attention not only to employee moral but also to the balance between change and continuity." [4]

---

[1] Huy (2001), p. 73.   [3] Huy (2001), p. 78.
[2] Huy (2001), p. 77.   [4] Huy (2001), p. 78.

6.4 Practices for Increasing Midmanager Involvement in Change

As in previous chapters, we conclude with seven actionable ideas that can be pursued to increase this particular dimension of organizational change capacity. While not all employees will welcome change, ignoring middle managers can have a devastating effect on change initiatives. In essence, involved middle managers are essential for bringing along a critical mass of employees to adopt a proposed change. As a result, middle managers' involvement in the design and execution of a change process is essential.

Practice 1: Accept the Differences between Middle Managers and Change Champions

In any organization, there are "A," "B," and "C" players. The A players are the ones who regularly exceed performance expectations and often step into leadership roles for change initiatives. They are the rising stars who have inordinate ambition, take risks, and like to push the envelope. The C players are those employees who are not meeting performance expectations. And then there are the B players. These are the employees who are meeting performance expectations, but they act in a supporting role to the rest of the organization. They assume a more "ordinary" and "limited" but critical role within the organization.

Within the middle management ranks, A players are often given most if not all the attention by senior management because they are often similar in drive and impact to those in senior executive positions. Often, these players are the change champions within the organization. In contrast, B players are often ignored and taken for granted while C players are given remedial attention or removed from the organization. Ignoring B players is a mistake since they play such a vital complementary role within a corporation. [1]

B players often place a higher value on work–life balance than do A players. B players may have second-rate educational backgrounds or technical skills compared with A players, but they compensate by developing extensive interpersonal skills or organizational memory. And B players often bring a depth of understanding to the organization and the unit in which they operate, since they have not progressed as quickly up the organizational ladder as have A players. [2]

Organizations need stars (i.e., A players) and a strong supporting cast (i.e., B players) if they want to be change capable. Senior executives need to recognize the differences between these two groups of employees and respect the differences in ambition, motivation, training, and so on. By understanding these differences, B players will feel more respected and involved and the organization will more likely benefit from their contributions.

Practice 2: Invest in Middle Manager Skills, Especially During Slow Periods

When the economy is growing robustly and the organization is hitting its performance targets, investing in manager development initiatives is relatively easy to do. However, during slow periods, most organizations suspend all professional development initiatives, especially for middle managers. This is a missed opportunity.

During slow periods, investing in human capital is an ideal time to enhance the skills of your middle management ranks. Slow periods bring about fear within the employees' ranks and present a unique opportunity to add new skills. By investing in management development initiatives for middle managers, the organization sends a signal that these employees are important, which reduces fear, and it generates loyalty. Furthermore, when the pace picks up, middle managers can sometimes rejuvenate their careers and display a burst of creative energy, become better supporting actors, or both. Management development is not a luxury during slow times, it is a necessity. [3]

Practice 3: Tailor Rewards to Things That Middle Managers Value

Not all middle managers want to become senior managers. Not all middle managers want to move every 2 to 3 years. Not all middle managers want to make huge sums of money. Not all middle managers want to tackle extremely challenging problems that have defied solution by others. Some middle managers are content with the way things are.

Most reward and recognition systems are designed to motivate and reward the A players. This needs to change. Change-capable organizations recognize the differences between A and B players and revise their reward systems to align with these differences. For example, rather than offering more compensation, sometimes the gift of time is valued as much if not more by some employees. Rather than offer a single career track, multiple career tracks should be considered since not all managers want the same careers and stress as do A players. In sum, recognize the differences between change champions and middle managers, and adjust your organizational systems to reward both types of management. [4]

Practice 4: Don't Ignore the Plateaued Middle Manager

Some middle managers provide solid and consistent performance, but they have plateaued in their careers. As a result, these plateaued managers are often older and less energetic than the change champions. However, with age sometimes comes wisdom and proven social networks and these individual capabilities are invaluable when the organization is confronted with large, transformative change initiatives. Perhaps this is why a recent research study found that the most effective managers in engaging with transformative change were the older, plateaued middle managers, as compared with the younger, rising stars. [5] Again, traditional middle managers can play a major supporting role and sometimes even a leading role in any change initiative.

Practice 5: Involve Middle Managers in the Strategy Formation Process

In today's increasingly information-based economy, successful strategy is more about learning faster than the competition than it is about exquisite and detailed deliberate strategic planning. Therefore, it only makes sense that involving the middle managers engaged with day-to-day operations as well as the customers can be a valuable source of learning and testing of strategic change ideas. Indeed, more and more research suggests that high-performance organizations regularly involve their middle managers in the substantive development of organizational strategy, as well as in its execution. [6] This involvement can be as formal and expensive as an organization-wide strategy conference, or as informal as a hallway chat with middle managers about the organization's external threats and opportunities. Whatever form it takes, engaging middle managers in forming the strategy as well as executing it will enhance their knowledge and commitment to future change programs.

Practice 6: Create a "Leadership Engine"

Adaptable and innovative organizations grow leadership at every level, and create a wide and deep array of internal talent to call upon in times of need. Leadership is not the preserve for a select few, but for as many in the organization as possible. This is especially true of middle managers who are not champions of change. Innovative organizations develop a "teachable point of view" on business ideas and values, and this can accelerate knowledge creation and transfer within the firm. Middle managers are not just "doers," they also are "thinkers." And if given the chance and the right circumstances, middle managers can also be "leaders." [7]

Practice 7: Enable Middle Managers to Constructively Challenge Senior Leaders

Many significant organizational disasters—such as the British Petroleum oil rig explosion or the Bernie Madoff Ponzi scheme— could have been prevented or mitigated if those in the middle management ranks were allowed to voice constructive criticism. Middle managers need to have access to the senior leaders and they need to be allowed to deliver news that is not flattering. As one organizational consultant puts it, "Followers and leaders both orbit around the (organizational) purpose; followers do not orbit around the leader." [8] In other words, organizations must cultivate courage in the middle management ranks to speak "truth to hierarchy," [9] and senior leaders need to be focused more on the well-being of the organization than on their own personal well-being. [10]

In sum, some of your middle managers need to be involved in helping to bring about change, even if they are not the change champions. Organization-wide change is complex and affects everyone. Middle managers can make a major contribution to actively bringing about change or passively assure its demise.

---

[1] DeLong and Vijayaraghavan (2003).

[2] DeLong and Vijayaraghavan (2003).

[3] Krishnamurthy (2008).
[4] DeLong and Vijayaraghavan (2003), p. 102.
[5] Spreitzer and Quinn (1995).
[6] Floyd and Wooldridge (1996).

[7] Tichy and Cohen (1997).
[8] Chaleff (2009), p. 13.
[9] Chaleff (2009), chap. 7, pp. 179–204.
[10] Judge (1999).

Chapter 7

Systems Thinking

A system must have an aim. Without an aim, there is no system. A system must be managed. The secret is cooperation between components toward the aim of the organization.

  - W. Edwards Deming

No problem can ever be solved with the consciousness that created it. We must learn to see the world anew.

  - Albert Einstein

7.1 A Primer on Systems Thinking

What Is a System?

W. Edwards Deming, the guru of total quality management, defines a system as "a network of interdependent components that work together to try to accomplish a common aim." [1] A pile of sand is technically not a system since the removal of a single component (i.e., a grain of sand) does not change the functioning of the collectivity (i.e., the pile). Furthermore, there is no "aim" designed into or emanating from the pile.

In contrast, a car is a system that comprises thousands of parts that all work together to provide transportation to a driver. If you remove the gasoline tank, then the car fails to perform its aim properly. In this case, the aim is designed into the car by the automobile design team, so the car is a mechanical, not a living, system.

Living systems are the most complex forms of systems. What makes them unique is that they interact with their environment and are self-organizing. As a result, the aim is not designed in but constantly evolving over time. Living systems can be something as simple as a cell, to something as complex as the European Union. Therefore, one of the ways of determining whether a collectivity is a system or not is (a) the interacting parts possess a central aim or purpose and (b) the removal of a component changes the functioning of the overall system. [2]

What Is Systems Thinking?

Systems thinking builds on our understanding of natural and man-made systems. It emphasizes that we need to understand how the whole affects its parts and how the parts affect the whole. This is different from traditional thinking, which assumes that the parts are independent of the whole. It is a set of techniques and an overarching mind-set that "problems" can best be solved by considering the component's relationship to the overall system and its environment.

This type of thinking is revolutionizing many fields of study. For example, we now know that the pain that you have in your back may be caused by one leg being longer than the other so that the skeletal subsystem is skewed. In other words, close examination of a person's back will reveal the symptoms (i.e., back pain), but not the causes (i.e., leg length differences). In traditional thinking, diagnosis of back pain focuses exclusively on the pained area of the body.

Systems thinkers tell us that there are two types of systems—closed and open systems. Closed systems function as systems relatively independent of their environment; open systems are constantly exchanging material, energy, and information with their environment. An example of a closed system is the circulatory system of a fish versus mollusks. In fish (and other vertebrates), the blood circulates within vessels of different lengths and wall thicknesses, so its circulatory system is relatively closed to the rest of its body cavities. In mollusks (and most invertebrates), there are no vessels and the blood circulates within the tissues of the entire body cavity. The key notion for our purposes is the fact that system openness is a relative state, not an absolute state.

Sometimes the components or elements of a system function as subsystems within a larger system. A subsystem is a collection of components or elements with a smaller aim within the larger system. Hence, there are various levels of systems that operate interdependently. A prime example here would be the financial subsystem's impact on and relationship with the larger national economic system.

The Organization as a Living System

Systems thinking is revolutionizing the organizational sciences, just as it is challenging all the other sciences. If we consider the organization to be a living system, then organizational problems and opportunities are viewed in an entirely new way. For example, a high-performing individual might be creating dysfunction within his or her work group. Similarly, an award-winning department might be the cause of organizational decline. And a financially successful organization could be polluting its natural environment.

Interestingly, systems thinking can lead to principles that transcend a particular area of study. For example, the Japanese often study natural systems (i.e., a river) to guide them in the design and improvement of interorganizational systems (i.e., a supply chain). Similarly, Margaret Wheatley has used systems insights from the study of quantum mechanics to better understand the proper functioning of organizational systems. [3]

Systems thinking requires us to consider the subsystems and components within an organization, and the organization as a subsystem within its larger environment. Organizations vary in terms of their levels of openness to the environment, and systems thinking suggests that a balance must be struck between maintaining some boundaries with the environment and assuring that those boundaries are somewhat porous. A classic systems problem is that the organization is not listening enough to its current customers (it is too closed), or that it is listening too much to its current customers, or what Clayton Christensen calls the innovator's dilemma. [4]

Systems thinking also requires us to consider the aim of the system and to what degree the members of the organization, or larger society, align with the overarching aim. Chris Argyris eloquently describes how individuals often have both espoused aims and actual aims; and how the key to individual health and productivity involves minimizing the distance between what is espoused and what is actual. [5]

The stakeholder versus stockholder perspective of organizations also deals with the aim of the organizational system. For some managers and theorists, maximizing shareholder wealth is the sole purpose of the corporation, and by doing so the overall economic system, of which the organization is a part, benefits. However, other managers and theorists suggest that there are multiple social actors inside and outside the organization with a "stake" in the functioning of the organization, and that no one stakeholder is more important than any other. Systems thinking enable managers to sort out this difficult, value-laden issue.

[1] Deming (1986), p. 32.
[2] Miller (1978).
[3] Wheatley (2006).

[4] Christensen (1997).
[5] Argyris (1993).

7.2 Systems Thinking and Organizational Change

Peter Senge was a pioneer in helping us to apply systems thinking to organizational change. He emphasized the central role of organizational learning, and created frameworks and tools for diagnosing organizational dysfunction and enhancing organizational functioning. In particular, he emphasized some of the organizational learning disabilities, or delusions, that must be acknowledged if the organization wants to change and survive.

The Delusion of Mental Models

Senge emphasizes that we all have mental models of how things work. When our organizations are not functioning properly, he suggests that we need to reconsider our individual and collective mental models. This is not easy to do because *mental models are deeply ingrained assumptions, generalizations, or even picture or images that influence how we understand the world and how we take action. Very often, we are not consciously aware of our mental models or the effects that they have on our behavior.* [1]

Therefore, change-capable organizations are conscious of their shared mental models, and are adept in revising those mental models when they no longer work properly.

The Boiled Frog Delusion

The boiled frog delusion is a commonly told story, but rarely do living systems learn from its message. If you place a frog in a pot of boiling water, it will immediately hop out. But if you carefully place the frog in a pot containing room-temperature water, and gradually raise the temperature of the water, the frog will not notice the temperature increase and will stay in the water even though he is free to jump out. The reason for this is that the frog's internal mechanism for survival is geared to deal with sudden changes to his environment, not gradual ones. The same applies to our organizations. [2]

In many ways, our organizations change dramatically and well when the environment shifts in radical ways. Think of how individuals and organizations in New York City demonstrated magnificent performance in the advent of the 9/11 terrorist attack, which was violent and sudden and dramatic. However, creeping problems like slowly eroding market share, insidious environmental pollution, steady quality declines, and turnover by some of the key employees of an organization are often not noticed. The environment is turning up the heat slowly but surely on many of our organizations, but it is happening so gradually that we do not notice or take action to correct this trend.

The Delusion of Learning from Experience

Most learning for individuals, organizational units, and overall organizations comes from reflection on the experienced effects that are the result of certain actions. For example, a common lesson learned within organizations is "When I deliver requested results on time and within budget, my project continues being funded." Or at the subunit level, "When our sales unit aggressively pursues new customers, sales grow for the company." And at the organizational level, "When our organization hits its earnings per share goal, our stock price rises."

However, what happens when there is not a direct effect of our actions on organizational outcomes? Many individuals recognize that they can do their best, but the project gets canceled for other reasons. And some sales units pursue customers aggressively and sales still fall. And some organizations hit their earnings guidance, but the stock price still continues to fall. When learning from direct experience doesn't work, Senge suggests that we need to think more systemically about cause and effect. He states, "Herein lies the core learning dilemma that confronts organizations: We learn best from experience but we never directly experience the consequences of many of our most important decisions." [3]

The Delusion of Individual Initiative within a System

When an individual or subunit within an organization is not meeting performance standards, the traditional response by the individual or subunit is to "work harder." Sometimes this works; often it does not. When this does not work, Senge points out that often the system is the problem, rather than the individual or individuals who are working within the system. Specifically, he states,

> *The systems perspective tells us that we must look beyond individual mistakes or bad luck to understand important problems…We must look into the underlying structures which shape individual actions and create the conditions where types of events become likely.* [4]

[1] Senge (1990), p. 8.   [3] Senge (1990), p. 25.
[2] Senge (1990), p. 23.   [4] Senge (1990), pp. 42–43.

7.3 Practices for Building Systems Thinking Into Your Organization

As in previous chapters, this concluding section lays out seven practices that are consistent with the chapter's focus, systems thinking, which can make your organization more change capable.

Practice 1: Try to Anticipate "Ripple Effects" of Change Initiatives

Unintended side effects are common with pharmaceuticals, so why should we be surprised when the same thing happens during or after an organizational change initiative is launched? Organizations are complex, interdependent social systems. Like a water balloon, when we push on one part of it, another part changes. While anticipating the side effects of a change initiative is not easy to do, some effort should be made to envision what those ripple effects might be.

Similar to scenario analysis of future environmental states, [1] by envisioning potential outcomes in advance we are more prepared to deal with the outcomes that may result. Furthermore, by trying to anticipate future unintended consequences, sponsors of the change and the change agents are more attentive to the unfolding nature of the change initiative and more likely to learn from the experience. [2] It is important to remember, however, that cause and effect are often not closely related in time and space when trying to change a complex system. Consequently, analogies can be a useful tool for anticipating unintended consequences of change. Another tool for anticipating the effects of a change initiative are computerized simulations. [3]

One systems thinking tool that can be instrumental in anticipating ripple effects are causal loop diagrams. [4] Diagrams help us to visualize how the change might unfold. Causal loops remind us that there are feedback linkages within systems that can dampen or amplify the effects of initiatives. In sum, anticipating ripple effects is more art than science, but the effort will ensure that unintended side effects are avoided and will deepen the change sponsors' understanding of the systemic nature of change.

Practice 2: Small Changes Can Produce Big Results; Search for Optimal Levers

There are no simple rules for finding high-leverage changes, but there are ways of thinking that make it more likely. Learning to see underlying "structures" rather than "events" is a starting point…Thinking in terms of processes of change rather than "snapshots" is another. [5]

Malcolm Gladwell wrote a best-selling book on this very topic and it was given the graphic term "tipping points." Gladwell argues that "the world may seem like an immovable, implacable place. It is not. With the slightest push—in just the right place—it can be tipped." [6]

Gladwell also asserts that ideas, products, messages, and behaviors can spread just like viruses do. Similar to how the flu attacks kids in schools each winter, the small changes that tip the system must be contagious; they should multiply rapidly; and the contagion should spread relatively quickly through a population within a particular system. Learning how your system has tipped in the past, and understanding who or what was involved can be an invaluable insight into thinking systemically about your organization.

Practice 3: Identify Feedback Loops and Multiple Drivers of Change

Systemic change often involves multiple feedback loops and drivers of change. As such, focusing on a single causal variable is often not helpful. For example, I often hear executives argue that "it is all about the right reward systems—get your rewards right and everything falls into place." While reward systems are very important and a key part of organizational change capability, they are a subsystem within a larger system that has many complex and interacting parts.

Barry Oshry writes insightfully about "spatial" and "temporal" blindness within an organizational system. Spatial blindness is about seeing the part without seeing the whole. Temporal blindness is about seeing the present without the past. Both forms of blindness need to be overcome in order to better understand cause and effect within a system. Oshry recommends that people from various parts of the system need to periodically take time out to reflect collectively so as to transcend their blind spots. [7]

Practice 4: Align Change Initiatives around an Inspiring Vision of the Future

Change is difficult and often painful. People generally will not give up an idea, behavior, or mental model without latching onto something to replace it. The something that they need to hold onto is the shared vision of the future. In their analysis of over 10,000 successful change initiatives in organizations, Jim Kouzes and Barry Posner found that the creation of an inspiring vision of the future was always present. [8] As Peter Senge notes, "When there is a genuine vision (as opposed to the all-too-familiar 'vision statement'), people excel and learn, not because they are told to, but because they want to." [9] And Jim Collins and Gerry Porras point out that "a visionary company doesn't simply balance between idealism and profitability; it seeks to be highly idealistic and highly profitable." [10] In sum, a compelling and well communicated vision is key to bringing about change within an organizational system, and this principle is central to systems thinking.

Practice 5: Seek to Change Associates' Mental Models

The definition of insanity is applying the same approach over and over again, and expecting new results—the same is true about mental models. When organizational changes don't work or when an organization repeatedly fails to meet its performance expectations, sometimes the dominant mental model, or paradigm, within an organization is to blame. Changing this dominant mental model is not easy since political capital is often tied up with particular models. First-order systems changes involve refinement of the system within an existing mental model. Second-order systems changes involve the unlearning of a previous mental model, and its replacement with a new and improved version. These changes do not occur on their own—second-order learning requires intention and focus on the history and identity of the overall system. [11]

Barry Oshry writes poetically about the "dance of the blind reflex." This reflex is a generalization of the mental models of various parts of the organizational system. Oshry argues that top executives generally feel burdened by the unmanageable complexity for which they are responsible. Meanwhile, frontline workers at the bottom of the organizational hierarchy feel oppressed by insensitive higher-ups. Furthermore, middle managers feel torn and fractionated as they attempt to link the tops to the bottoms. Furthermore, customers feel righteously done-to (i.e., screwed) by an unresponsive system. Interestingly, none of the four groups of players mentioned see their part in creating any of the "dance" described here. [12] However, there is a way out of this problem. As Oshry notes,

> We sometimes see the dance in others when they don't see it in themselves; just as they see the dance in us when we are still blind to it. Each of us has the power to turn on the lights for others. [13]

Peter Vaill uses the metaphor of "permanent white water" as an analogy for the learning environment that most organizations currently find themselves in. He argues that "learning to reflect on our own learning" is a fundamental skill that is required for simple survival. Vaill argues that learning about oneself in interaction with the surrounding world is the key to changing our mental models. He further suggests that the personal attributes that make this all possible are the willingness to risk, to experiment, to learn from feedback, and above all, to enjoy the adventure. [14]

Practice 6: Engage in Vigorous Dialogue around the Welfare of the System

Dialogue aimed at understanding the organizational system is fundamental to enhancing systems thinking. This dialogue should involve top executives, middle managers, frontline workers, and customers at repeated intervals. Organizational systems gurus, such as Deming, Senge, and Oshry, all agree that the key to systemic thinking is to involve a wide variety of voices within the system talking and listening to each other. Town hall meetings, weekend retreats, and organizational intranets are a common and increasingly popular means of engaging in dialogue about the system.

Practice 7: Work to Maintain Openness to the System to Avoid Entropy

When an individual or group within the system engages with another individual or group within the system that is "not normal"; new information is created within that system. External to the system, when an individual or group engages with individuals, groups, or other organizations that are not normal, new information is created between the systems. This new information can lead to energy and matter transfer that counteracts systemic entropy.

Intrasystemic openness occurs when two departments agree to collaborate on a project that contains mutual benefits to each. "Open door" policies are clearly a step in the right direction. Even a simple act of going to lunch with someone you have never dined with before can reduce system entropy. Extra systemic openness occurs when new employees are hired, when external consultants are engaged, and when individuals attend trade association meetings or external training sessions. The human tendency to stick with the known and familiar and maintain routine must be challenged by the continual creation of new connections.

In sum, a systemic perspective is essential for making your organization change capable. Systems thinking is an infrastructure within which all change takes place.

[1] Schwartz (1991).

[2] Schriefer and Sales (2006).

[3] Ziegenfuss and Bentley (2000).

[4] Hebel (2007).

[5] Senge (1990), p. 65.

[6] Gladwell (2002), p. 259.

[7] Oshry (1996), p. 27.

[8] Kouzes and Posner (2003).

[9] Senge (1990), p. 9.

[10] Collins and Porras (1994), p. 44.

[11] Gharajedaghi, 2007.

[12] Oshry (1996), p. 54.

[13] Oshry (1996), p. 123.

[14] Vaill (1996), p. 156.

Chapter 8

Communication Systems

The single biggest problem in communication is the illusion that it has taken place.
  - George Bernard Shaw

Good communication is as stimulating as black coffee, and just as hard to sleep after.
  - Anne Morrow Lindbergh

8.1 Communication Challenges in Modern Organizations

All communication involves the transmission of a message from a sender to a receiver. Communication is central to organizational effectiveness and survival because the essence of organizations is cooperation, and no cooperation is possible without effective communication. [1] While communicating effectively has never been easy to do in organizations, there are some special challenges to communication in today's organizations.

Information Overload

Every organization must solve the problem of what pattern of communication shall be instituted, and what information shall be directed to what offices. One issue in establishing such a pattern is information overload. There are limits to the amount of communication that can be received, coded, and effectively handled by any one individual. [2]

John Kotter has an interesting anecdote that illustrates this problem. He asserts that the typical employee receives approximately 2,300,000 words or numbers communicated to him or her in a 3-month period. He estimates that the typical communication of a change vision over 3 months is one 30-minute speech, one hour-long meeting, one 600-word article in the firm's newspaper, and one 2,000-word memo, which amounts to about 13,400 words. Consequently, roughly one-half of one percent of all the words or facts that an employee receives over 3 months will be focused on the change vision. [3]Clearly, routine information can easily overwhelm change messages.

Sterility of Electronic Communication Technologies

We live in a time of disruptive electronic technologies, some of which have led to new and powerful information and communication technologies. Data-based reporting systems, e-mail, voice mail, intranets, bulletin boards, Websites, and video conferencing are cost effectively breaking down large distances and providing information to huge numbers of people in relatively inexpensive but fast ways. Unfortunately, these mediums of communication are rather sterile and impersonal, and not as powerful or meaningful to people as more personal modes of communication.

Because change initiatives can arouse strong and passionate emotions within an organization, these marvelous information and communication technologies are often not up to the task. Since visual cues are so important in all human communication, non-visual mediums disconnected from context, such as e-mail, just don't communicate well. Since human relationship is so important to communication, mediums that do not add to the relationship, such as electronic bulletin boards, can convey different messages to different receivers. And since impersonal "digital" communication is relatively fast and easier to do than more personal communication forms, senders are often not as practiced or as skilled in the more personal modes. In sum, electronic communication systems are invaluable to today's organizations, but they have considerable limitations when it comes to bringing about change.

[1] Barnard (1938).
[2] Katz and Kahn (1966), p. 257.

[3] Kotter (1996), p. 89.

8.2 Organizational Communication and Change

Due to the aforementioned reasons, as well more traditional communication problems such as sender arrogance or receiver resistance to change, change initiatives often fail to meet their objectives. For instance, John Kotter flatly states that ineffective communication of the change vision is one of the primary causes of failed organizational transformations. [1] T. J. Larkin and Sandar Larkin, two noted communication consultants, assert that change-oriented communications are too often lofty, vague, and impersonal so the message is never really understood and therefore change initiatives founder. [2] And Rob Goffee and Gareth Jones observe that most change communication lacks authenticity, so the rest of the organization doesn't trust what is being said and consequently the change effort stalls or goes in unintended directions. [3]

Unfortunately, there is much more written about how communication fails to support change than what works. Consider the title of one article arguing for more communication within organizations: "If communication isn't working, nothing else will." [4] In another article, a leadership expert states,

Transformation is impossible unless hundreds of thousands of people are willing to help, often to the point of making short-term sacrifices. Employees will not make sacrifices, even if they are unhappy with the status quo, unless they believe that useful change is possible. Without credible communication, and a lot of it, the hearts and minds of the troops are never captured. [5]

Also, many change consultants point out how pervasive rumor and innuendo are within organizations today due to the ineffective communication at work. For example, Jeannie Duck states, "In the absence of communication from the leaders, the organization will seek information from other sources, whether those sources know what they are talking about or not. Your silence does not stop conversation; it just means you are not participating in it." [6]

Unfortunately, many if not most of the communication prescriptions made tend to be overly simplistic or overly complex. On the simplistic side, some observers argue that all change communications simply need to be face-to-face, frequent, and informal. [7] While these practices have merit, they do not consider such contextual factors as the organization's size and geographic diversity, the urgency of the change initiative, or the availability of communications technology.

On the other hand, some change communication prescriptions are overly complex. For example, one change consultant recommends that a formal change communication action plan be developed for every change initiative. These action plans were recommended to include (a) careful consideration of change targets, (b) deliberate change messages, (c) prespecification of change messages, (d) timing and frequency of the message(s), (e) establishment of ownership for the communication, and (f) measurements planned for the change. Of course, then the change leaders are supposed to execute this plan and iterate as necessary. [8] One wonders if the change leaders will have any time to do anything other than communicate to the rest of the organization!

[1] Kotter (1996).

[2] Larkin and Larkin (1994).

[3] Goffee and Jones (2006).

[4] Taylor (1998).

[5] Kotter (1995), p. 60.

[6] Duck (2001), p. 143.

[7] Anastasiou (1998).

[8] Bennett (2000).

8.3 Using the Communication System to Bring About Change

One of the primary reasons why communication within organizations tends to be fragmented is that the organizational leaders think of it as a collection of tools rather than an overall system. [1] An organization's communication system consists of a particular message, the change leader(s) personal attributes, the change targets' collective readiness to change, feedback loops between leader(s) and target(s), and the variety of channels of communication operating within an organization. Robust organizational communication systems are essential for bringing about organizational change. The following section discusses each aspect of the communication system.

The Change Message

When communicating with others, it is important to consider the nature of the message in order to make sure that it is heard. For example, downsizing and layoff messages evoke strong and often powerful emotions within organizations. Consequently, the timing and medium of that message should be tailored to address the delicate nature of the information intended. Similarly, the message must be clear and direct if there isn't much time to make the change. And if the message is complicated, such as the need to replace an old technology with an entirely new one, then the communication system must take this into consideration. [2]

Change Leader Attributes

If the change leader is perceived to be honest and authentic, then the message is likely to be heard—no small task in our information overload world. Authentic leader(s) display their true selves throughout the changes of context that require them to play a variety of roles. Authentic leaders also nurture their relationship with followers by highlighting their strengths, while revealing human weaknesses; they maintain their individuality while conforming enough to hold the organization together, and they establish intimacy with followers while keeping enough distance to command respect. [3]

Related to the notion of authenticity is the ability of the change leader to listen well. Warren Bennis and Bert Nanus state, "A leader must be a superb listener, particularly to those advocating new or different images of the emerging reality. Many leaders establish both formal and informal channels of communication to gain access to these ideas." [4]

A third and final characteristic of the change leader is his or her credibility with the rest of the organization. As we discussed in the trustworthy leadership dimension, credibility brings trust. What we add in this chapter is that this credibility-induced trust also facilitates communication and information sharing.

Followers' Readiness to Change

Employees within an organization vary in their readiness to change. Some individuals just don't like any change, while others will leap at the opportunity to try something new. Most individuals vary between these two poles of readiness depending on the perceived costs and benefits of a particular proposed change. In other words, if the employee perceives a change as relatively easy to adopt (i.e., low cost), and the change brings about many advantages or solves existing problems (i.e., high benefit), then the employee will be relatively open to the change. [5]

Another way to think about the employee's readiness to change is to consider all change proposals as a diffusion-of-innovation problem. Everett Rogers devoted his lifetime to understanding how innovations diffused within social systems, and he discovered a very interesting fact: When confronted with a particular change, individuals tend to sort themselves out into a normal distribution in terms of readiness to change. In other words, roughly 16% of all employees will be early adopters of proposed changes; 34% will then follow the early adopters. Next, another 34% of employees will be late adopters. And finally, 16% of the employees will resist the proposed change as long as possible. [6] In sum, when attempting to communicate to an entire organization, it is very helpful to know something about the nature of the change targets before, during, and after a change initiative is launched.

Feedback Loops

Most systems have feedback loops, and communication systems are no exception. Just because a change message is issued is no guarantee that the message is heard. Furthermore, even if the message is heard at the time that it is issued, it may not be remembered later on. And even if the message is remembered, it may not lead to new behavior. Hence, feedback loops are essential for uncovering what was heard, what was remembered, and what new behaviors, if any, have resulted.

In addition to message assessment, feedback loops are also helpful in improving the change initiative, for a variety of reasons. First, the change designers may not see the entire situation, and feedback loops help them to broaden or refine their perspective. Second, some change initiatives are just wrong-headed, and the communication system should enable the rest of the organization to weigh in on its overall worth and efficacy. Finally, new things are learned as change initiatives are rolled out, and these lessons need to be distributed to the rest of the organization so that the lessons can be leveraged.

Barry Oshry points out that most feedback loops within organizations are "filtered" so that the established reality perceived by senior management, middle managers, or frontline workers goes unchallenged. Furthermore, in complex social systems, such as an organization, feedback loops often provide conflicting information. When this happens, most social systems tend to ignore the information because sorting out the discrepancies can be difficult, upsetting, and time consuming. [7] Effective communication systems have many feedback loops, and the information conveyed as feedback is weighed and considered.

Channels of Communication

There are a wide variety of communication channels possible within organizations. Communication channels involve both formal and informal mediums of information exchange. Formal mediums include such things as town hall meetings, newsletters, workshops, videos, e-mail, bulletin boards, manuals, roadshows, and progress reports. [8] Informal mediums include such things as hallway discussions, one-on-one meetings, departmental briefings, and having senior leaders walking the talk. In both cases, the invisible social network within the organization plays a powerful role in interpreting the message. [9]

While most organizations tend to prefer using certain communication channels in all situations, the selection of the channel should be based on the specific change context. The reason for this is that communication channels vary in their efficiency and information richness. Rich communication channels are typically interactive and face-to-face, and they provide an abundance of contextualized information. Some channels, such as e-mail, are extremely efficient but not information rich at all. Other channels, such as one-on-one private meetings, are not efficient at all, but extremely information rich. In general, the more complicated and emotionally charged the change initiative, the more communication channels will be needed, and they need to be information rich, particularly in the beginning of the change program.

[1] Katz and Kahn (1966).

[2] Kotter (1996).

[3] Goffee and Jones (2006).

[4] Bennis and Nanus (1997), p. 96.

[5] Armenakis, Harris, & Mossholder (1993).

[6] Rogers (1983).

[7] Oshry (1993).

[8] Balogun and Hailey (2008), p. 195.

[9] Farmer, 2008.

8.4 Practices of Good Communication Systems

Once again, we conclude our chapter discussion with seven action items that can be pursued to develop this particular dimension of organizational capacity for change. These suggestions are not comprehensive, but research and common sense suggest that they can work to enhance your communication system.

Practice 1: Hire, Develop, and Retain Effective Communicators

In a 1998 survey of 480 companies and public organizations by the National Association of Colleges and Employers, communication abilities are ranked number one among personal qualities of college graduates sought by employers. Work experience and motivation are second and third. [1] Clearly, one of the reasons why communication skills are so important is that these skills are essential for facilitating organizational change. A less obvious reason why good communicators are essential is that these individuals understand how to design and enhance the communication systems within an organization so that information flows more effectively.

For example, Rob Goffee and Gareth Jones argue that effective leaders "communicate with care." Communicating with care means that the leaders choose their channels of communication strategically, tailor their message to the aims of the change initiative, authentically disclose intimate details when appropriate, and are very sensitive to the pace and timing of their communications. [2] Clearly, any employee with this subtle set of skills is a rare and valuable human resource, and the organization does well to enhance this skill set in as many individuals as possible, since their skill can be leveraged into improved communication systems for the entire organization.

Practice 2: Invest in Information Technologies and Experiment with New Formats

The number one capital investment for most organizations is in information technologies; the primary new means of communicating within organizations. By some accounts, information technologies account for 35% to 50% of all business capital investment in the United States. [3] There are several obvious reasons for this high level of investment—the clear benefits of productivity gains due to improved information, the transition from an industrial to an information-based economy, and the declining cost of information technologies coupled with increasing capabilities.

However, information sharing is the essence of communication, and so effective information technologies are an essential ingredient to making an organization change capable. Information is being shared more extensively with not only senior executives but also with the entire organization. Examining trends in information sharing in trying to understand organizations that were "built to change," Ed Lawler and Chris Worley reported that of the five common types of information within an organization, all were being shared with a wider range of employees. The five typical types of information being shared were (a) corporate operating results, (b) unit operating results, (c) new technologies, (d) business plans and goals, and (e) competitor's performance. Interestingly, more than half of all employees in all organizations received regular information in these five areas in 2005; whereas in 1987, only corporate and unit operating results were reported to half of the employee base. [4]

Effective information systems do the following six things for an organization to make it more change capable. First, they provide comprehensive data on key processes. Second, these systems integrate data across departmental boundaries. Third, they monitor organizational capabilities as well as performance. Fourth, they are linked to goal setting and reward systems, which are central to organizational change. Fifth, they include information on customer and competitors. And finally, effective information systems make measurements visible throughout the organization. [5] Clearly, good communication is not likely to occur without good information, and effective information technologies are a necessary ingredient to make that happen.

Practice 3: Talk the Walk and Walk the Talk

There is nothing more devastating to change initiative and overall change capability than for the senior leaders to espouse the benefits of change and then not act in alignment with those espoused benefits. In other words, when the behavior from prominent people within an organization is inconsistent with the change vision, then all other forms of communication are disregarded. [6] In short, "walking the talk" is an essential part of the communication system within an organization.

This process begins with the chief executive of the firm modeling the behavior being sought by the change vision. Next, it requires the top management team to police themselves to act congruently with the change vision. And if there are sponsored change agents by the senior executive team, these individuals clearly need to "walk the talk" as well. Change leaders are in a fish bowl, and they must be as if not more willing than the rest of the organization to change their behaviors. As Mahatma Gandhi stated, "Be the change you wish to see in the world."

Practice 4: Use Stories, Metaphors, Analogies, and Pictures as Much as Possible

Effective communication systems connect the hearts and minds of the rest of the organization. Stories, metaphors, and analogies are powerful ways to communicate complex information in compelling ways. John Kotter emphasizes that this is particularly important for communicating the change vision. He restates the truism that "a verbal picture is worth a thousand words."[7]

However, figurative communication in the form of verbal pictures or graphic depictions is also essential for building confidence in the change program. Stories are pithy narratives with plots, characters, and twists that are full of meaning. Leaders are discovering that the telling of actual "success stories" can often be the catalyst for momentum behind a change initiative. [8] Metaphors and analogies are inferential techniques to transfer the meaning of something that is known to another thing that is unknown. For example, Plato compared our perception of reality to shadows on the wall of a cave. Darwin used diagrams of trees to help explain his theory of evolution. And Shakespeare saw the world as a stage. [9] Organizational change, by definition, requires employees to try something new and move into the unknown. Communication systems that rely on stories, metaphors, and analogies can make the unknown future state more attractive and understandable.

Practice 5: Repeat the Message Many Times in Many Forums, but Keep It Fresh

It is common for change leaders to announce a new change program and pull out all the stops to communicate it to the rest of the organization in the early part of the change initiative, only to move onto other pressing issues after it has been launched. This is a mistake, and it leads to the change cynicism that pervades many organizations today. Furthermore, organizational changes take time to adopt, often years, and this requires focused attention on the part of the rest of the organization.

Consequently, the change message must be repeated many ways in many different contexts using multiple communication channels. [10] However, this does not mean that daily e-mails with the same message need to be sent out to the entire organization. It does mean that creative and different versions of the same message need to be distributed periodically in various channels. For example, the change vision could be communicated to large and small groups in formal and informal ways at the launch of a major change program.

Furthermore, forums for listening to the employees' reactions to the change need to be set up, and sometimes the change initiative needs to be adjusted. Furthermore, progress reports on implementing the change program can be circulated electronically or visually. Paycheck stuffers might provide factoids that related to the proposed change. And town hall meetings can be used to discuss the change initiative to those who have complaints to voice, are curious, or both. As Marshall MacLuhan noted, "the medium is the message," [11] so repeated, pervasive, and fresh change messages help to gain the attention, interest, and eventual adoption of an information overloaded workforce.

Practice 6: Seek to Discuss the Undiscussable

In every organization, there are undiscussable issues. An undiscussable issue is a taboo subject, something people in an open forum don't talk about in order to avoid an emotionally charged discussion. These issues are undiscussable because people are fearful of releasing "negative" emotions that could jeopardize working relationships. (What some people express colorfully as "naming the elephant in the room.") Common undiscussables are challenging an existing reality, questioning those in power, sharing concerns about an idea that is being sold as "perfect," or simply agreeing to disagree when perspectives clash. [12]

In addition to emotionally charged undiscussables, there are also logical inconsistencies that need to be addressed by the communication system. Organizational change is complicated and there are often inconsistencies when moving from one organizational state to another. If the communication system does not address these inconsistencies, then the credibility of the entire change initiative is called into question. [13] Furthermore, it is much more honest and productive to discuss undiscussables. [14]

There are a wide variety of ways to successfully discuss the undiscussables, but it all starts with having an attitude of seeing everyone as being in partnership around the success of the overall system. [15] Therefore, blaming leaders or employees is usually not constructive, but structuring in debate and conflicting viewpoints is. Being defensive is rarely helpful, but being curious is. Avoiding discussions of delicate issues will hold back progress, but playful and humorous treatments of tricky issues can help. Emphasizing individual responsibility to the exclusion of collective responsibility clearly leads to an imbalance. Sometimes enabling anonymous discussion of undiscussables using Web-based technologies can shine a light on "the elephant in the room." [16]

Practice 7: Leverage Informal Social Networks

A social network is "the structure of personal and professional relationships you have with others. Social capital is the resources—such as ideas, information, money, and trust—that you are able to access through your social networks." [17] Social networks and capital exist inside and outside of the organization, but the internal organizational networks can be most powerful in dealing with organizational issues. Informal social networks consisting of simple things like friendships outside of work or regular lunch gatherings during work can have a major influence on change implementation success. Unlike the formal organizational structure, the informal social network is nonhierarchical, constantly evolving, and essentially based on trust, reciprocity, and common values. The informal social network complements the formal organizational structure of an organization.

It is a mistake to communicate only through the formal organizational structure. Indeed, Peter Drucker observed that in more than 600 years, no society has ever had as many competing centers of power as today. In addition, he noted that as we move to a more knowledge-based economy, informal social networks are increasingly important to organizational success and survival. [18]

Informal social networks in the form of ad hoc peer groups can spur collaboration and unlock value as well as thwart collaboration and destroy value. If internal social networks are ignored, they can be a source of role conflict, rumor mongering, resistance to change, and conformity of thought and action. If they are successfully leveraged, they can complement the formal organization, be more fluid and responsive, and magnify the impact of advocates of change. Consequently, in order to leverage the social network, the first order of business is to be aware of it, and the second priority is the attempt to influence it so that the organization can more effectively enhance its communication system.

In sum, effective communication systems are an essential element of any change capable organization. These systems complement the systemic thinking dimension in such a way that the knowing-doing gap is bridged. [19]

[1] Bennett (2000), p. 73.
[2] Goffee and Jones (2006).
[3] Anonymous (2010).
[4] Lawler and Worley (2006), p. 123.
[5] Lawler and Worley (2006), pp. 125–126.
[6] Kotter (1996), p. 90.
[7] Kotter (1996), p. 90.
[8] Denning (2007).
[9] Wormeli (2009).
[10] Kotter (1996), p. 90.
[11] McLuhan (1964).
[12] Hammond and Mayfield (2004).
[13] Kotter (1996), p. 90.
[14] O'Toole and Bennis (2009).
[15] Oshry (1996).
[16] Hammond and Mayfield (2004).
[17] Carpenter (2009), pp. 5–6.
[18] Drucker (1992).
[19] Pfeffer and Sutton (2000).

Chapter 9

Accountable Culture

It is not only what we do, but also what we do not do, for which we are accountable.

- *Moliere*

Only entropy comes easy.

- *Anton Chekhov*

9.1 What Does It Mean to Be Accountable?

Accountability refers to an obligation or willingness to accept responsibility for one's actions. When a person accepts responsibility, that person is committed to generating positive results, what some people call "taking ownership." Sometimes responsibility is obligated by assuming a specific role within an organization. For example, the chief financial officer of a corporation is obligated for knowing about and protecting the financial well-being of the firm. However, lots of work gets done within organizations for which the person is not obligated. For example, that same chief financial officer might demonstrate concern for the natural environment even though he or she is not formally responsible for it.

When individuals are accountable, they understand and accept the consequences of their actions for the areas in which they assume responsibility. When roles are clear and people are held accountable, work gets done efficiently and effectively. Furthermore, constructive change and learning is possible when accountability is the norm. When roles are not clear and people are not held accountable, work does not get done properly, and learning is not possible.

In highly litigious societies, such as the United States, accountability is often hard to assign or constructive to assume since there is a lot of societal downside to being responsible and not much upside. This is particularly true for organizational actions whereby an individual does not have full control over the outcomes. For example, individuals are often eager to serve on a board of directors as it is a prestigious position that can lead to new learning and an expanded network with other elites. However, board members are often quick to disavow responsibility for many organizational dysfunctions when class action lawsuits get filed. Avoidance of accountability is not only bad for society; but it is also devastating for organizations. And since accountability can be the container in which organizations change occurs, it is essential to organizational capacity for change.

9.2 Organizational Culture and Accountability

Clearly, supervisors are the ones who possess the authority to hold employees accountable for results; and the board of directors is the group responsible for holding the senior-most executive accountable. However, managers and directors vary in their interest and ability to do this. Consequently, cultivating an organizational culture that supports and encourages accountability within an organization is fundamental to organizational change.

What Is an Organizational Culture?

While there are many definitions of organizational culture, I think that one of the clearest was offered by Edgar Schein. He defined organizational culture as

> *a pattern of basic assumptions—invented, discovered, or developed by a given group as it learns to cope with its problems of external adaptation and internal integration—that has worked well enough to be considered valid and, therefore, to be taught to new members as the correct way to perceive, think, and feel in relation to those problems.* [1]

Schein argued that there are three levels of culture in any organization. The most visible level of culture is where observable organizational artifacts such as technology, art, dress, pictures, architecture, and audible behavior occur. A cultural artifact is a term used to refer to any observable item or action created by humans that gives information about the collectivity of the creators, the users, or both. The intermediate level of organizational culture is the values and beliefs about what the purpose of the organization is, and what gives meaning to its existence. Usually, there is a social consensus as to what values and beliefs matter most within an organization. And finally, at the deepest unconscious level within an organization, there are assumptions about human nature, human relations, time, and the organizational and environmental interface. Schein argued that these assumptions serve as the foundation for the values, norms, and beliefs within all organizations, and are hardest to change. [2]

Some observers argue that organizational culture can be a "social control" mechanism that is more efficient and effective than more formal and traditional control mechanisms due to its fluid pervasiveness. [3] However, a more common view is that organizational culture is the "social glue" that makes organizational life meaningful. [4]

In recent years, organizational culture has emerged as a key source of competitive advantage for many firms. Since resources can be easily obtained by new entrants, technology can be easily copied by competitors, and employees are now highly mobile, traditional ways of generating competitive advantage through industry positioning are less relevant today. Furthermore, it has been increasingly observed that a strong set of core values and beliefs often leads to competitive advantages and superior performance for many firms. Since performance above industry norms is a common indicator of competitive advantage, organizational culture is getting more attention by strategists. Finally, since culture is relatively hard to imitate, the competitive advantage is often sustainable. [5]

How Cultural Norms Influence Accountability Behaviors

In many organizations, there is not a cultural focus on being accountable and getting results. Indeed, five "crippling habits" deeply embedded in an organizational culture are (a) absence of clear directives, (b) lack of accountability, (c) rationalizing inferior performance, (d) planning in lieu of action, and (e) aversion to risk and change. [6]

There are many explanations for these negative habits. One is that senior executives consciously or unconsciously neglect their responsibility for executing the strategy well. Forming a brand new strategy is exciting, garners attention from external stakeholders, and happens rather quickly. In contrast, executing an existing strategy requires attention to detail, is often not noticed outside of an organization, and takes a long time to manifest an effect. Hence, making an organization accountable is often not "sexy" to senior leaders. [7]

Another reason why organizational cultures do not hold members accountable is what is known as the "smart talk trap." This phenomenon refers to organizational cultures that emphasize talk over action, looking good over getting results, and sounding intelligent rather than delivering results. Managers sometimes let talk substitute for action because that is what they have been trained to do. In addition, there is a human propensity to assume intelligence for those who talk with complex words and focus on hard-to-understand concepts. Unfortunately, complex words and concepts are often difficult to execute. And finally, studies have shown that individuals who criticize ideas are often judged to be smarter than individuals who attempt to be helpful and constructive. While critical thinking is clearly needed in organizations, it often does not lead to constructive action. [8]

Whatever the reason for lack of accountability within an organization, organizational cultures are central to making the organization change capable. Indeed, there is a "hard side" to change management and it centers on keeping people accountable and getting organizationally important results. Prescribing desired results, clarifying responsibility, measuring performance, rewarding those who meet or exceed expectations, and challenging those who do not are all integral to an organization's norms, values, and assumptions about the way things get done. Accountability is a cultural mind-set, and accountable behaviors emerge from organizational cultures that value it.

---

[1] Schein (1985), p. 9.
[2] Schein (1985), p. 14.
[3] Ouchi (1980).
[4] Alvesson (2002), p. 32.

[5] Barney (1986).
[6] Prosen (2006).
[7] Bossidy and Charan (2002).
[8] Pfeffer and Sutton (1999).

9.3 Cultural Accountability and Organizational Capacity for Change

Two books have become popular tomes on the relationship between cultural accountability and organizational capacity for change. The first book, written by Larry Bossidy and Ram Charan, talks about the importance of creating a culture focused on executing strategy well. Bossidy and Charan note that execution must be a core element of an organization's culture and that execution is a discipline that is essential to strategic success.

Larry Bossidy quickly rose through the management ranks at General Electric, and then inherited a turnaround situation when he became CEO at Honeywell International. He states,

> *My job at Honeywell International these days is to restore the discipline of execution to a company that had lost it. Many people regard execution as detail work that's beneath the dignity of a business leader. That is wrong. To the contrary, it's a leader's most important job.* [1]

Bossidy goes on to say, "Organizations don't execute unless the right people, individually and collectively, focus on the right details at the right time." [2]Since Bossidy led Honeywell through a very successful and dramatic turnaround, his words carry special weight.

The second major book devoted to creating accountability was written by three change consultants—David Ulrich, Jack Zenger, and Norm Smallwood. They argue that many leaders and leadership training courses neglect the fact that leadership is about getting desired results. In their own words,

> *Results-based leaders define their roles in terms of practical action. They articulate what they want to accomplish and thus make their agendas clear and meaningful to others. Employees willingly follow leaders who know both who they are and what they are doing. Such leaders instill confidence and inspire trust in others because they are direct, focused, and consistent.* [3]

Furthermore, they argue that accountability is the primary means for achieving those results. They state,

> *Organizations may learn, change, and remove boundaries, but if they lack accountability and discipline, success will elude them over time. Accountability comes from discipline, processes, and ownership. Discipline requires getting work done with rigor and consistency, meeting scheduled commitments, and following through on plans and programs to deliver promises. Process accountability may require reengineering how work gets done, reducing redundant efforts, and driving down costs at every level. With accountability comes ownership, as individuals feel responsible for accomplishing work. Leaders who foster accountability continuously improve how work gets done, deliver high-quality products and services, and ensure commitment from all employees.* [4]

In sum, change-capable organizations benefit from cultures of accountability. In the next section, I provide some ideas for making your culture more accountable.

[1] Bossidy and Charan (2002), p. 1.

[2] Bossidy and Charan (2002), p. 33.

[3] Ulrich, Zenger, & Smallwood (1999), p. 21.

[4] Ulrich, Zenger, & Smallwood (1999), p. 97.

9.4 Practices for Making Your Organizational Culture More Accountable

Organizational cultures are very difficult to change and it takes considerable time to do so. The organizational founder and previous experiences of an organization help to establish "how things get done around here"; and these norms, values, and assumptions are often not conscious or easily changed.

However, cultures are particularly sensitive to the behaviors and attitudes of senior leaders. Therefore, senior leaders do have a special interest and responsibility in reinforcing positive and productive aspects of a culture, and replacing negative and unproductive aspects. Furthermore, due to the intangible and relatively intransigent nature of culture, productive cultures can be a source of sustained competitive advantage. The following are seven different things that can be done to make your culture more accountable. Since a culture consists of the artifacts, values, and assumptions that drive organizational action, changing a culture needs to involve change in all three areas. Listed below are seven principles that can assist you in making your culture more accountable for results.

Practice 1: Begin with a Focus on Results Being Sought

Effective accountability means that there is a clear understanding of the results being sought throughout the entire organization. This requires intense thought and ongoing dialogue about what the organization's purpose is, and what it is trying to achieve. It starts with a clear understanding of the overall mission of the organization and then cascades down into performance standards expected for each and every individual within that organization. Without asking the question as to "what is wanted" before deciding how to do it, organizational members who act without full knowledge of the results required may work harder but accomplish less. [1]

Accompanying this clarity on results is the clarity of the goals being sought. Sometimes, organizational goals are ambiguous and unenforceable, what some call "resolutions." While resolutions may sound good, the actions required are often not clear and the results being sought can be up to interpretation. Clear goals, on the other hand, specify what is desired and by when. And when individuals commit to clear goals, positive outcomes emerge. [2]

Practice 2: Assign Responsibility for Results to Everyone in the Organization

If your organization has difficulty assigning responsibility for results, consider responsibility charting. This technique is essentially a matrix with results desired in one column, and individuals in an organizational unit in the other columns. Matrix entries specify who is responsible for what and, if possible, when results are expected. With this relatively simple approach, responsibility and clarity is much clearer, especially if there is a review of the results achieved when compared with the results desired.

But not all responsibility can be assigned in advance. Sometimes individuals volunteer to be accountable for certain results in special circumstances. Stories are an effective tool for eliciting volunteers to become more accountable, particularly when the story involves a previous member of the organization who overcame overwhelming odds to deliver extraordinary results. Success stories are part of every culture, and success stories about accountability help to make the culture more accountable as well as encourage volunteerism. [3]

In your attempt to be clear about responsibility, effective communication is essential. Sometimes leaders know exactly what they want, but they don't communicate clearly what is desired. Sometimes leaders have a vague idea of what is wanted and dialogue needs to be conducted with subordinates to help clarify matters. When the dialogue is open, candid, and informal, clarity ensues and accountability results. [4]

Practice 3: Leaders Should Demonstrate the Behaviors That Align With the Proposed Change

Culture change starts and gains momentum with changed behavior on the part of the leaders of that organization or organizational unit. Nothing kills a change initiative faster than leaders who espouse certain behaviors and attitudes, but demonstrate different ones. For example, if a leader announces the importance of controlling costs more carefully, but then he or she arranges for a lavish executive retreat or decorates his or her office in excessive ways, the rest of the organization takes notice. Hence, leaders need to exercise care in the behaviors they exhibit. [5]

In addition, leaders need to be careful as to behaviors that they tolerate. If results are being stressed and their subordinate does not deliver results, then there needs to be demonstrable consequences. This applies to both meeting the numbers and behaving consistently with the organization's values. Indeed, it has been observed that if a nonperformer gets high enough in the organizational hierarchy and is not held accountable, that person can literally destroy the organization. [6]

Practice 4: Measure the Right Performance Standards and Do It Rigorously

It is a skill to link desired results and goals with standards and metrics of performance. If a performance standard is done well, achievement of that standard will realize the results being sought. Designing realistic timetables and appropriate performance standards is not easy to do well, and it is particularly difficult for large, complicated projects. And for those change initiatives that have an extended time horizon, intermediate milestones must be set with care. Nonetheless, rigorous standard setting is an essential activity if an accountable culture is being sought. [7]

Clearly, performance measures need to be balanced or else the organization risks becoming unbalanced. Consequently, this suggests that multiple performance standards are required. However, if the performance standards are too numerous, then assessing performance is no longer possible. Overall, focusing on a relatively few, balanced performance standards works best for making the organization more accountable. [8]

When designing performance standards, it is sometimes helpful to distinguish between ends and means standards. When the strategic goals are established and measureable, then metrics that focus on the end result are most appropriate. However, when the strategic goals are changing and not easily measured, then metrics that focus on the means for bringing about the change are most appropriate. In either case, however, measurements can and should be applied. [9]

Finally, most people assume that utilizing performance standards implies a bureaucratic organization; however, this does not have to be the case. Accountability can be achieved in nonhierarchical organizational structures when it comes from within the employee or is reviewed in nonbureaucratic ways. [10]

Practice 5: Make Sure That Cultural Artifacts Support Accountability

As discussed previously, cultural artifacts are the visible expressions of the underlying values and assumptions that pervade an organization. When changing a culture, changing the visible artifacts makes a conscious and unconscious impression on the organization's members. There are at least five types of cultural artifacts: (a) normal behavior, (b) myths and sagas, (c) language systems and metaphors, (d) symbols, rituals, and ceremonies, and (e) physical surroundings including interior design and physical equipment. [11]

One cultural artifact surrounding accountability is who gets celebrated and who gets ignored. Clearly, celebrating and promoting individuals who deliver results on time and within budget is one way to support movement to more accountable culture. Also, individuals who don't deliver results on time or within budget need to be privately confronted, coached, and sometimes removed from the organization. [12]

The transformation of Continental Airlines is a prime example of how important changing artifacts are to making a culture more accountable. To change behavioral norms that had been associated with low productivity, the leaders instituted a bonus system that rewarded high levels of productivity. In order to align the culture with the new business strategy, the leader's next act was to reduce the corporate policy manual from 800 pages to just 80 pages and then conduct a ritual where the former manuals were burned by the employees. In addition, the catch phrase "from worst to first" was used to focus employees' attention on the desired results. Whenever key milestones were achieved, corporate celebrations were arranged. And executives were required to work on holidays so that "we are all in this together" in Continental's effort to become more accountable and productive. And the repainting of the jets, renovating of the gateways, and purchasing of state-of-the-art information technology all contributed to the turnaround initiative. [13]

Practice 6: Discuss Assumptions Underlying Actions Dealing With Accountability

The fastest but perhaps most challenging way to change an organizational culture is to change the assumptions underlying that culture. Since culture is the "taken-for-granted" way of doing things within an organization, this is not an easy task. However, change-capable organizations are adept at naming the assumptions underlying organizational actions and changing those assumptions when they no longer serve the organization.

Surfacing and debating assumptions is the means by which cultural change is achieved, and paying attention to assumptions around accountability is a key way to make your organization more change capable. Larry Bossidy and Ram Charan note,

> *Debate on assumptions is one of the most critical parts of any operating review—not just the big-picture assumptions but assumptions specifically linked with their effects on the business, segment by segment, item by item. That's a key part of what's missing in the standard budget review. You cannot set realistic goals until you've debated the assumptions behind them.* [14]

Practice 7: Make Sure That the Reward System Focuses on Accountability

A key aspect of accountability means that there are consequences to meeting or not meeting performance standards. This suggests that the reward and recognition system needs to celebrate and reward those who consistently deliver results and develop a reputation for accountability, and it needs to confront and punish those who consistently fail to deliver results. [15]

Many organizations do a good job celebrating and recognizing good performance. Very few organizations deal with nonperformers well even though this is a key process for any organization that takes accountability seriously. Most employees like knowing where they stand in terms of performance, and the performance evaluation system is central to making an organization accountable. It is particularly important that the performance evaluation system is based on hitting predefined targets and standards as much as possible. However, care must be exercised in selecting the right standards, not just those that are easiest to measure. [16]

In the absence of rigorously defined standards, performance evaluation becomes more focused on nonperformance criteria. Since each organization is unique, customized reward and recognition systems are becoming the norm for organizations seeking greater accountability. [17]

In sum, creating and maintaining a culture of accountability is essential to bring about a change-capable organization. This does not mean that organizations need to measure everything and become more mechanical. If thoughtfully developed, however, measurements and responsibility assignments can aid in organizational learning and adaptability.

[1] Ulrich, Zenger, & Smallwood (1999), p. 21.
[2] Heath and Heath (2008).
[3] Wines and Hamilton (2009).
[4] Bossidy and Charan (2002), p. 102.
[5] Bossidy and Charan (2002), p. 105.
[6] Bossidy and Charan (2002), p. 115.
[7] Osborne (1993).
[8] Ulrich, Zenger, & Smallwood (1999).
[9] Melnyk, Hanson, & Calantone (2010).
[10] Ulrich, Zenger, & Smallwood (1999), p. 97.
[11] Shrivastava (1985).
[12] Bossidy and Charan (2002).
[13] Higgins and McAllaster (2004).
[14] Bossidy and Charan (2002), p. 236.
[15] Kerr and Slocum (2005).
[16] Kerr (1975).
[17] Heneman, Fisher, & Dixon (2001).

Chapter 10

Innovative Culture

The achievement of excellence can only occur if the organization promotes a culture of creative dissatisfaction.
 - Lawrence Miller

Everything that can be invented has been invented.
 - Charles H. Duell, Director of U.S. Patent Office, 1899

10.1 What Does It Mean to Be Innovative?

Organizations in all developed economies (and increasingly many developing economies) want to be innovative. While cost control, cost parity, or both are important to be competitive, organizations in developed economies simply cannot compete with the low cost advantages that developing economies offer. As a result, more and more organizations voice or attempt to embrace the 21st-century mantra, "Innovate or die." [1]

Many people equate creativity with innovation, and while this is understandable it is also a mistake. Creativity is the process of generating something new; while innovation is the application of creativity to a new product or service that has value. Product innovations add direct value to customers; process innovations add indirect value to customers by lowering costs, increasing the quality of new or existing products, or both. Value is generated by taking a creative new idea and moving it through a series of stages in order to yield a practical new innovation. Therefore, creativity is a necessary, but not sufficient condition for innovation.

Another misconception about innovation is that it is effortless and just happens. The philosopher Plato observed that "necessity is the mother of invention." This observation suggests that problems are the stimulus for creativity and innovation and that persistence is required. Perhaps this is why T. S. Eliot, the highly creative American writer, stated, "Anxiety is the hand maiden of creativity"; and Andy Grove, the highly successful CEO who guided the Intel Corporation through an amazing streak of innovative activity, insists that "only the paranoid survive." [2] In sum, creativity and innovation are essential for just about any organization today, but they are different concepts and neither comes easily.

[1] Peters (2006).   [2] Grove (1996).

10.2 What Makes an Organizational Culture Innovative?

In this chapter, I argue that the key to making an organization innovative is to cultivate an innovative culture, our eighth and final dimension of organizational capacity for change. There are many reasons why creative ideas and innovative projects are killed within organizations. Notably, almost all of them have to do with an overweighting of the risks to existing operations, and an underassessment of the returns associated with new ideas based on the overarching organizational culture. Clearly, not all ideas should be pursued and the pursuit of new ideas needs to be selective.

However, very few organizations know how to fully explore new ideas and develop the best ideas into innovative new ventures. Perhaps that is why the stock market values Apple so highly, due to its rare ability to keep coming up with a steady stream of innovative new products and services year after year.

"The creative process is social, not just individual, and thus forms of organization are necessary. But elements of organization can and frequently do stifle creativity and innovation." [1] Organizational cultures become creative and innovative when they encourage "combinatorial play." [2] In other words, employees need to imaginatively combine ideas in new ways and then play with them to see how the new combination works in reality. In most organizations, however, imagination and play are not valued, getting work done on time and under budget is; pursuing ideas with unproven merit is frowned upon; and extrinsic rewards are emphasized over intrinsic rewards. All of these traditional cultural norms and values thwart the development of innovation since creative employees usually value imagination and play and pursuing new ideas into unknown realms, and are highly motivated by intrinsic rewards.

A second aspect of organizational culture that is fundamental to creativity is the cultivation of diversity of thought. Although many organizations pay lip service to the need to diversify their workforce, diversity of observable demographic traits is typically the emphasis, not diversity of thought. When the workforce is highly diverse, then misunderstandings are likely, conflict often ensues, and productivity can decline. Clearly, none of these outcomes is a pleasant experience and they do not automatically lead to innovations. However, if diversity of thought is welcomed in an organizational culture, creativity and innovation are more likely. [3]

A third aspect of organizational culture that can facilitate innovation is the ubiquity of weak ties. Strong ties are relationships we have with family members, close friends, and longtime neighbors or coworkers. They tend to be ties of long duration, marked by trust and reciprocity in multiple areas of life. In contrast, weak ties are those relationships that are more on the surface—people we are acquainted with but not deeply connected to. Research has shown that creative individuals have many "weak ties" inside and outside their work organizations. [4] Consequently, organizational cultures that encourage flexible working conditions and external networking make innovation more likely. Hence, there is a spontaneous and serendipitous aspect to innovative cultures.

A fourth aspect of organizational culture that nurtures creativity and innovation is an organization-wide ability to look long term. Today's organizations are very lean and short-term focused. They are so busy exploiting existing markets, they don't have the time or resources or capacity to explore new markets. However, organizational cultures that enable the organization to both exploit and explore markets make it possible for its leaders to "fly the plan while rewiring it." [5]

A fifth aspect of organizational culture that makes creativity and innovation possible is the tolerance of ambiguity and failure. As Woody Allen states, "If you are not failing every now and again, it's a sign you're not doing anything very innovative." Clearly, not all new ideas will work out as hoped, so ideas that lead to dead-ends are an inevitable part of the innovation process. Unfortunately, most organizational cultures seek to blame individuals who fail, rather than accepting occasional failures and attempting to learn from the experience.

A sixth aspect of organizational culture stems from the reality that most innovations come from collaboration within and across teams, not the genius or perseverance of a single individual. For example, in a scientific study of R&D units in the biotechnology industry, Judge and associates found that the most innovative units operated more like goal-directed communities than as a collection of big-name scientists. [6] Nonetheless, many organizations seek to hire employees who are extremely intelligent, come from prestigious universities, or both, and these are often the individuals who have the most problems collaborating with others.

[1] Florida (2002), p. 22.

[2] Shames (2009).

[3] Basset-Jones (2005).

[4] Granovetter (1973).

[5] Judge and Blocker (2008).

[6] Judge, Fryxzell, & Dooley (1997).

10.3 Innovative Cultures and Capacity for Change

Some executives believe that the key to being innovative is all about investing heavily in a Research and Development unit; others argue that all innovation stems from hiring the right leaders; still others assert that innovation is largely a matter of luck and serendipity. However, the research consensus is that organizational culture is the primary source of comprehensive and sustained innovation. [1] The primary reason for this is that innovation is a teachable discipline that involves many different people in collaboration. [2]

There is a wide variety of cultural typologies in the organizational sciences, but one of the most popular is the "Competing Values" framework advanced by Kim Cameron and Robert Quinn. According to these authors, there are four classical types of organizational cultures: (a) hierarchy, (b) market, (c) clan, and (d) adhocracy. These four organizational cultures vary in their relative emphasis on flexibility and discretion bestowed upon individuals and their external focus on variation and differentiation. The "adhocracy" culture is reported to be the one cultural type that is most conducive to innovation since it emphasizes flexibility and discretion over stability and control and external differentiation over internal integration. [3]

As Cameron and Quinn point out, some cultures are more open to innovation and change than others, but the reason for this is that there are competing values tugging the culture in multiple directions. The "hierarchy" culture, with its inward integration coupled with a stability and control focus, is the exact opposite of the adhocracy culture. Indeed, hierarchical cultures are useful for addressing matters of accountability, as discussed in the previous chapter. However, too much emphasis on control and an overly inward focus will limit the overall capacity for change of the organization. In sum, there must be a balance struck between innovation and accountability for those organizations that seek to expand their capacity for change.

Innovation is fostered by information gathered from new connections, from insights gained by journeys into other disciplines or places; from active, collegial networks and fluid open boundaries. Innovation arises from ongoing circles of exchange, where information is not just accumulated or stored, but created. [4]

Clearly, the more open the culture is to new ideas and connections, the more likely that it will be innovative and capable of change.

In 2004, *Fast Company* magazine nominated W. L. Gore and Associates as "pound for pound, the most innovative company in America." They argued that their impressive string of innovations were a direct result of their culture, which was designed specifically to be innovative. What is striking is how nonhierarchical Gore's culture is. For example, they emphasize the power of small, interdisciplinary teams over formal organizational structure. There are no ranks, no titles, and no bosses to report to. The firm takes the long view as much as possible; and it emphasizes the importance of face-to-face communication. Associates are encouraged to spend up to 10% of their time pursuing speculative new ideas. And the culture celebrates failure in order to encourage risk taking. [5]

[1] Garvin (2004). [4] Wheatley (2006), p. 113.
[2] Drucker (1993). [5] Deutschman (2004).
[3] Cameron and Quinn (1999).

10.4 Practices for Making Your Culture More Innovative

Similar to previous chapters, we conclude this chapter with a discussion of seven practices that can be used to enhance your organization's capacity for change in this particular area.

Practice 1: Make Innovation Everyone's Responsibility

In too many organizations, innovation is assumed to be the responsibility of the top management team, or the research and development unit. [1] While these two groups of people are essential, this emphasis will fail to capture the "wisdom of the anthill." [2] Innovation is essentially a collaborative endeavor, where collective imagination yields new business opportunities. [3]

According to Peter Drucker, innovation and entrepreneurship are capable of being presented as a discipline. In other words, it can be learned and practiced. Most important for us in this chapter, Drucker asserts that it can be fostered and encouraged throughout an entire organization. [4] One of the keys appears to be to create a collaborative, "information-rich" environment in which all employees are invited to contribute. [5] Commenting on the success of the Sundance Film Festival, Robert Redford stated, "If you create an atmosphere of freedom, where people aren't afraid someone will steal their ideas, they will engage with each other, they will help one another, and they will do some amazingly creative things together." [6]

Practice 2: Hire and Retain Creative Employees

All innovation depends on the generation of new ideas, but no new ideas will be generated in the absence of human creativity. Consequently, the hiring process needs to emphasize the importance of selecting individuals who have creative potential. More importantly, the human resources system needs to focus on developing that creativity and retaining individuals who show creative promise. [7]

However, creative individuals aren't the only ones required to cultivate a more innovative culture. Other individuals, such as "knowledge brokers," are also essential. Knowledge brokers are individuals who constantly collect ideas and combine them in unique and valuable ways. They often are not the originators of the ideas, but they have a skill at keeping new ideas alive and seeing where they lead. [8] Sometimes older workers lose their creative spark but serve as knowledge brokers to keep the spark alive.

Most organizations are uncomfortable with "mavericks" who shake up the status quo and display irreverence for accepted wisdom. However, mavericks play a vital role in making an organization more innovative, especially larger organizations. [9] For example, Jack Welch, a relatively famous maverick who led General Electric through a very innovative period, stated, "Here at GE, we reward failure." [10] Indeed, there is scientific research that demonstrates that when the reward system recognizes and retains creative employees, the organization behaves more innovatively. [11]

Practice 3: Put as Many Promising Ideas to the Test as Possible

A popular but controversial mantra in innovative organizations is "fail fast, fail cheap." The idea here is that it is important to get your new ideas in rough form out into the marketplace, and learn from your customers. This is in contrast to the "go–no go" approach where companies want new ideas to be 95% right before taking any action. [12] Perhaps this is why IBM's Thomas Watson, Sr., once said, "The fastest way to succeed is to double your failure rate." [13]

However, fast and cheap are not enough; the innovative organization also needs to learn from the experience in order to make the "failure" pay off. This is where testing comes in. Hence, a key ingredient to becoming more culturally innovative is the importance of designing relatively small-scale, but rigorous tests or "experiments." For example, Capital One, a highly successful retail bank, was founded on experimental design where new ideas were constantly tested. Tests are most reliable when many roughly equivalent settings can be observed—some containing the new idea and some not. [14] Similarly, IDEO, perhaps the most innovative design firm in the world, is a staunch proponent of encouraging experimenters who prototype ideas quickly and cheaply. [15] In sum, innovative cultures fail fast and fail cheap and learn from their failures.

Practice 4: Use Your Human Resources System to Create Psychological Safety

Organizations operate in increasingly competitive environments. The concept of "winning" is an important one, and being labeled a "winner" is usually a key to organizational advancement. Unfortunately, failure is an integral part of innovation, so innovative cultures need to create the psychological safety whereby failure in certain circumstances is acceptable. [16]

Some mistakes are more lethal than others, so mistakes that do not jeopardize the survival of the organization need to be accepted, even welcomed by leaders. Relatedly, it is more important to focus on the ideas rather than the individuals behind the ideas so that failure is not personalized. And "failure-tolerant leaders emphasize that a good idea is a good idea, whether it comes from Peter Drucker, Reader's Digest, or an obnoxious coworker." [17]

Once again, the human resources system can be instrumental in helping to create the psychological safety to enable innovation. In this case, the system can be designed to permit and even celebrate failure. [18] Clearly, this involves a balancing act between rewarding success and tolerating failure. Consequently, the key is to create sufficient psychological safety within a culture so that the organization can "dance on the borderline between success and failure." [19]

Practice 5: Emphasize Interdisciplinary Teams throughout the Entire Organization

In the 1970s and 1980s, many organizations tried to create specialized subunits where their mandate was to make the organization more innovative. This structural approach to innovation largely failed, either immediately or in the long term. For example, General Motors created the Saturn division as a built-from-scratch innovative new way to produce and sell cars. At first, Saturn had spectacular success. However, the lessons learned from Saturn never translated to the rest of the organization and recently the Saturn division was eliminated. [20] Similarly, too many large organizations try to rely solely on their research and development units for innovation, which greatly constrains the idea production and development process. [21]

Innovation is clearly a team sport, one that should pervade the entire organization. As a result, ad hoc interdisciplinary teams appear to be the proper structural approach to fostering innovation.

Today, IDEO is one of the most innovative firms in the world, and their approach to business is centered around interdisciplinary teams. [22] In sum, the ad hoc interdisciplinary team appears to be the structural solution to innovation, not a self-contained innovative subunit as some suggest.

Practice 6: Change Cultural Artifacts and Values to Signal Importance of Innovation

Recall from the previous chapter that one key way to change a culture is to intentionally shift the cultural artifacts in the direction of the desired change. When creativity and innovation is desired, it is important to be more flexible in the work environment. So flexibility in working arrangements, dress codes, and organizational titles becomes important.

New myths and rituals are required that focus on creativity and innovation. For example, some organizations celebrate failed experiments based on imaginative new ideas. Other organizations promote individuals who took a risk on a promising new idea that did not work out. And changing the formal values statement to incorporate an explicit statement about creativity and innovation highlights its new importance. Still others change the metaphors used in the organization. For example, creating a "blank canvas" culture evokes an image of artists operating without artificial constraints.

Fundamentally, cultures are not changed by new thoughts or words, they are changed by new behaviors that reinforce the cultural attributes that are desired. For example, GM's automobile plant in Fremont, California, transformed its culture by adopting the lean manufacturing behaviors advocated by its new venture partner, Toyota Motors. For example, nothing was as transformative at this particular plant as the "simple" act of empowering frontline employees to stop the productive line at any time due to quality concerns. This new policy had dramatic impacts on the revitalization of this unionized plant. [23]

Practice 7: Change Cultural Assumptions to Signal Importance of Innovation

Culture change does not occur until the underlying assumptions that pervade the organization are challenged and replaced with some new assumptions. Therefore, ordering new behaviors isn't enough. The organization must thoughtfully identify what the old assumptions are and work to instill new assumptions that support the culture desired. Consequently, contemplation and reflection are essential to any culture-change initiative. Perhaps this is why Gary Hamel and C. K. Prahalad note that "true strategy is the result of deep, innovative thinking." [24]

Some observers call for "disciplined reflection"; [25] while others urge leaders to identify "constraining assumptions." [26] Whatever the term that is used, organizational members need to think deeply about where their culture limits innovation, and to identify what cultural assumptions are the limiting factor. This requires a collective perspective; very rarely can a single leader come to this realization. Since most organizations have a bias for action, this reflection can be especially difficult. However, organizational learning often requires unlearning old and harmful assumptions and this is especially true for cultivating innovativeness. [27]

In conclusion, the eighth and final dimension of organizational capacity for change is an innovative culture that fosters and celebrates creativity and innovation. This dimension is an essential counterbalance to accountability systems. Together, these two dimensions complete our understanding of how to make your organization more change capable.

[1] Hargadon and Sutton (2000).

[2] Hamel and Prahalad (1994).

[3] Hammer (2004).

[4] Drucker (1996).

[5] Kanter (2006).

[6] Zades (2003), p. 67.

[7] Mumford (2000).

[8] Hargadon and Sutton (2000).

[9] Stringer (2000).

[10] Farson and Keyes (2002).

[11] Chandler, Keller, & Lyon (2000).

[12] Hall (2007).

[13] Edmondson (2002), p. 64.

[14] Davenport (2009).

[15] Kelley and Littman (2005).

[16] Edmondson (2008).

[17] Farson and Keyes (2002), p. 70.

[18] Bowen and Ostroff (2004).

[19] Wylie (2001).

[20] Hanna (2010).

[21] Stringer (2000).

[22] Kelley and Littman (2005).

[23] Shook (2010).

[24] Hamel and Prahalad (1994), p. 56.

[25] Edmondson (2008).

[26] Hammer (2004).

[27] Senge (1990).

Chapter 11

The Big Picture

In this concluding chapter, we take a look at the big picture that surrounds organizational capacity for change. Specifically, this entails (a) looking at the centrality of organizations in our lives, (b) distilling the eight dimensions of organizational capacity for change into four organizational attributes, and (c) providing some ideas and tools for assessing your own organization.

11.1 The Centrality of Organizations in Our Lives

We live in an organizational society today. All of us have memberships in multiple organizations, and the effectiveness of these organizations probably varies greatly. Ralph Kilmann, an astute academic and organizational consultant, captures these sentiments well:

Organizations are the greatest invention of all time. They enable people to transcend their own limitations of both body and mind in order to manage the problems of natures and civilizations. Without organized activity, all the other great inventions either would not have been created, or would have been brought to the marketplace. It is hardly an overstatement to suggest that economic prosperity and quality of life for the people of the world are largely determined by the functioning of organizations and institutions. [1]

Since organizations are so central to our lives and since they are so important to the fate of humanity, it is imperative that they function well. However, the organizations of the 21st century are not agile enough to deal with the unpredictable and increasingly volatile nature of the environments that they occupy. We need organizations that are more capable of change. This book is dedicated to that premise.

---

[1] Kilmann (1989), p. ix.

11.2 Four Organizational Attributes of Change-Capable Organizations

Two Human Capital Attributes: Organizational Trust and Lateral Leadership

Recall that there are eight dimensions of organizational capacity for change. The first four dimensions focus on the human capital within your firm. These dimensions focused on your human capital are depicted in Figure 11.1 "The Human Capital Required for Organizational Capacity for Change". The first two dimensions, trustworthy leadership and trusting followers, are oriented toward producing organizational trust to the greatest extent possible. Organizational trust refers to the ability of members of an organization to put their lives and well-being at risk in service to the well-being of the overall organization. Hence, it refers to how much frontline workers trust middle managers and senior executives to watch out for their interests. Similarly, it addresses how much top executives trust middle managers and frontline workers to do their jobs well. Trust suggests that we perceive the other as not only competent but also genuinely concerned about the general well-being of others. [1]

The second two dimensions, capable champions and involved midmanagement, are oriented toward unleashing the power of lateral leadership. Lateral leadership is concerned with getting things done across organizational units and functional areas of expertise. [2] The hierarchical organization will always be with us, but the power of hierarchical authority is diminishing. In its place is the power of influence without authority, in other words, lateral leadership. Crisis situations demonstrate this power quite clearly. When a crisis occurs, people often self-organize into social groups that do amazing things in inexplicably short amounts of time. The trick here is to enable the organization to self-organize. In this book, I have emphasized the importance of creating change champions and involving middle management in the change process so that lateral leadership can occur. Figure 11.1 "The Human Capital Required for Organizational Capacity for Change" contains a graphical depiction of the two organizational attributes dealing with human capital in change capable organizations.

Two Social Infrastructure Attributes: Systemic Knowledge and Cultural Ambidexterity

Organizations also require adequate social infrastructure in order to be change capable. Social infrastructure is the means by which organizational members come to understand and deal with the life of the overall organizational system. One key attribute that is part of the social infrastructure is the level of systemic knowledge within the organization. Systemic knowledge is the degree to which members of an organization understand and are focused on the overall organizational system. Too often, members focus on just their careers or just their organizational subunit. When a critical mass of the organization becomes focused on the overall life of the organizational system, the organization becomes much more open to the environment. This openness translates into more agility and flexibility within the system. [3]

Figure 11.1 The Human Capital Required for Organizational Capacity for Change

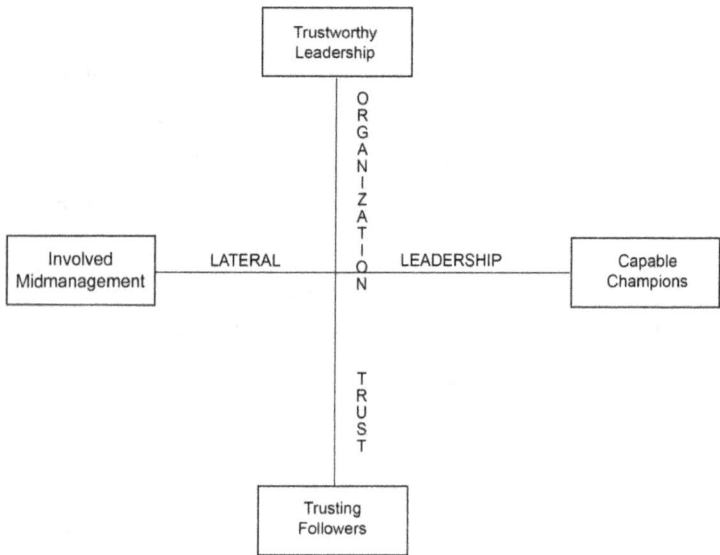

The fourth and final organizational attribute that is fundamental to change capability is cultural ambidexterity. Many observers note the powerful role that organizational culture plays in facilitating or thwarting organizational change. What is often missed, however, is that change-capable organizations balance accountability with innovation. If the organization overemphasizes accountability, innovation suffers. And if innovation is the sole focus, accountability is ignored. Change-capable organizations optimize on both of these seemingly contradictory cultural virtues. [4] Hence, the organization needs to become ambidextrous culturally, using the right-handed accountability norms in balance with the left-handed innovation norms. [5]

[1] Gilbert (2005).
[2] Fisher and Sharp (2004).
[3] Oshry (1996).
[4] Quinn (1991).
[5] Judge and Blocker (2008).

11.3 Assessing Your Organizational Capacity for Change

If you are now convinced that organizational capacity for change is an important capability that you want to develop in your organization, this final section contains some ideas for assessing your organization's capacity. There are two ways that your organization's capacity for change can be assessed. First, you can do this qualitatively by interviewing individuals at various levels of the organization and attempting to characterize it along these eight dimensions in narrative format using anecdotes and stories to illustrate where the organization stands. Second, you can do this quantitatively by administering an anonymous survey to the entire organization and aggregating the numerical results.

Appendix A contains a reliable and valid instrument that you can use to quantitatively assess your organization's change capacity. [1] This instrument can be administered online or via paper and pencil to any strategic business unit within your organization. [2] It is best if you administer the survey to your entire organization since a census provides the clearest picture of where the overall organization stands. However, sometimes a census is just not feasible. In these cases, it is necessary that a random sampling approach be taken. Appendix B illustrates that these items are reliable as shown through the relatively high factor loadings across the eight dimensions derived from a statistical factor analysis. For further reading about the reliability and validity of this instrument, please consider reading the publication that covers this issue. [3] In previous research using this instrument, I have discovered that it is important to sample sufficient numbers of senior executives, middle managers, and frontline employees within the organization. The reason for this is that, in general, top management often has the most optimistic view of the organization's capacity for change, and frontline workers have the most pessimistic viewpoint. Interestingly, the middle managers' viewpoint is typically in between these two assessments, and the gap between the midmanagement and senior-level perspective tells you how much work is required to enhance the change capability. Therefore, it is important to collect a representative sample of individual perceptions from the top, middle, and bottom of the organizational hierarchy.

Once you have collected the data from tops, middles, and frontline workers, it is useful to aggregate that data by the three levels and for the overall organization. If you are graphically minded, it can be helpful to construct a radar chart depicting the eight dimensions of organizational capacity for change by adding up the mean score for the four items in each dimension. Since a minimum score would be 4 across the four items and a maximum score would be 40, your organizational score will be somewhere between these two extremes. As can be seen in Appendix C, descriptive statistics are provided for each of the eight dimensions for the over 200 strategic business units that have been previously assessed using the instrument in Appendix A. Notably, *Communication Systems* is often the lowest evaluated dimension of the eight, and *Trustworthy Leadership* is typically the highest evaluated dimension. This suggests that improving your communication before, during, and after change initiatives offers the biggest opportunity for improvement. In addition, it is interesting to point out that the coefficient of variation is highest for *systems thinking* and *communication systems*, which suggests that strategic business units vary the most on these two dimensions.

Appendix D contains the mean values across the three hierarchical subgroups of employees required to assess organizational capacity for change. As might be expected, senior executives consistently rate the organizational capacity for change the highest, and frontline workers consistently rate it the lowest. In all cases except for accountable culture, middle managers rate the dimensions of organizational capacity for change in between these two subgroups. Overall, this benchmark data can be used to compare your organization to a wide variety of organizations operating in a wide variety of industries throughout the world.

A final worthwhile assessment is to track your organizational capacity for change over time. This can be done by administering the instrument at one point in time, and collecting data at a later point in time. Some organizational leaders choose to do this at regular intervals (e.g., every year, every quarter); other organizational leaders choose to do this after a major intervention event (e.g., following a post-acquisition integration program or a major training program). Armed with longitudinal data, you get a perspective as to whether your organization is improving in its overall capacity for change.

---

[1] This survey instrument can also be used as an interview protocol for qualitative interviews.

[2] Sometimes organizations are so large, and comprise so many organizational units, that it does not make sense to assess capacity for change for the entire organization. Hence, meaningful assessments are made at the strategic business unit level. A strategic business unit is an organizational subunit with profit and loss responsibility, or a cost center within an organization. For smaller, single-business organizations, the strategic business unit is the entire organization.

[3] Judge and Douglas (2009).

11.4 Concluding Thoughts

Figure 11.2 The Social Infrastructure Required for Organizational Capacity for Change

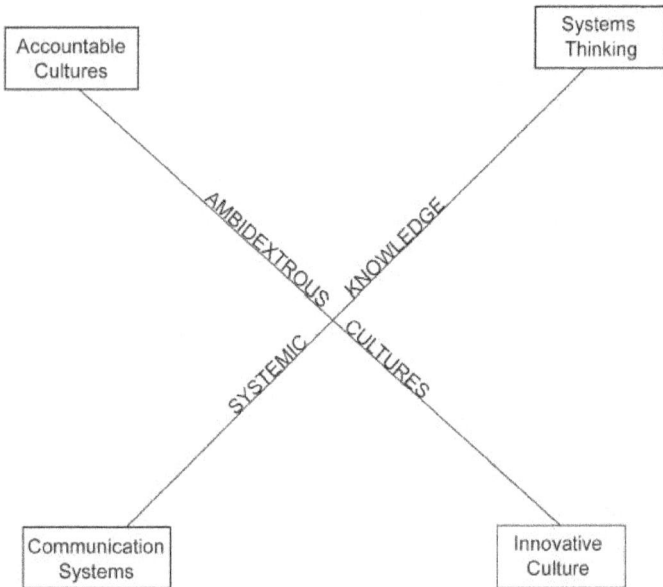

Organizations in the 20th century were built for stability and predictability. Organizations in the 21st century need to be both stable and change capable, what some refer to as "dynamically stable". [1] As a result, many organizations today tend to be overmanaged and underled as we transition to a global, information-based economy. This book provides insights, research, practical suggestions, and an approach to systematically assess your organization's capacity for change using a valid and reliable survey instrument. Both management and leadership are essential skills required for 21st century organizations. This book provides some insights that can enable your organization to survive and prosper in the new millennium.

---

[1] Abrahamson (2000).

Appendix A

Organizational Capacity for Change Survey Instrument

Item #	Question	Almost never			Sometimes			Always		
	Do the unit leader(s)									
01	protect the core values while encouraging change?	1	2	3	4	5	6	7	8	9	10
02	consistently articulate an inspiring vision of the future?	1	2	3	4	5	6	7	8	9	10
03	show courage in their support of change initiatives?	1	2	3	4	5	6	7	8	9	10
04	demonstrate humility while fiercely pursuing the vision?	1	2	3	4	5	6	7	8	9	10
	Do we have an organizational culture that									
05	values innovation and change?	1	2	3	4	5	6	7	8	9	10
06	attracts and retains creative people?	1	2	3	4	5	6	7	8	9	10
07	provides resources to experiment with new ideas?	1	2	3	4	5	6	7	8	9	10

Item #	Question	Almost never			Sometimes				Always		
08	allows people to take risks and occasionally fail?	1	2	3	4	5	6	7	8	9	10
	Does information flow effectively										
09	from executives to workers?	1	2	3	4	5	6	7	8	9	10
10	in a timely fashion?	1	2	3	4	5	6	7	8	9	10
11	across organizational units?	1	2	3	4	5	6	7	8	9	10
12	from customers to the business unit?	1	2	3	4	5	6	7	8	9	10
	Do middle managers in this organizational unit										
13	effectively link top executives with frontline employees?	1	2	3	4	5	6	7	8	9	10
14	show commitment to the organization's well-being?	1	2	3	4	5	6	7	8	9	10
15	balance change initiatives while getting work done?	1	2	3	4	5	6	7	8	9	10
16	voice dissent constructively?	1	2	3	4	5	6	7	8	9	10
	Do frontline employees										
17	open themselves to consider change proposals?	1	2	3	4	5	6	7	8	9	10
18	have opportunities to voice their concerns about change?	1	2	3	4	5	6	7	8	9	10

Item #	Question	Almost never			Sometimes				Always		
19	generally know how change will help the business unit?	1	2	3	4	5	6	7	8	9	10
20	generally view top management as trustworthy?	1	2	3	4	5	6	7	8	9	10
	Do employees throughout the organizational unit										
21	experience consequences for outcomes of their actions?	1	2	3	4	5	6	7	8	9	10
22	meet deadlines and honor resource commitments?	1	2	3	4	5	6	7	8	9	10
23	accept responsibility for getting work done?	1	2	3	4	5	6	7	8	9	10
24	have clear roles for who has to do what?	1	2	3	4	5	6	7	8	9	10
	Do change champions recognize the										
25	interdependent systems implications of change?	1	2	3	4	5	6	7	8	9	10
26	importance of institutionalizing change?	1	2	3	4	5	6	7	8	9	10
27	need to realign incentives with desired changes?	1	2	3	4	5	6	7	8	9	10
28	value of addressing causes rather than symptoms?	1	2	3	4	5	6	7	8	9	10
	Do we have change champion(s) who										

Item #	Question	Almost never			Sometimes				Always		
29	command the respect of the members in the unit?	1	2	3	4	5	6	7	8	9	10
30	possess good interpersonal skills?	1	2	3	4	5	6	7	8	9	10
31	are willing and able to challenge the status quo?	1	2	3	4	5	6	7	8	9	10
32	have the will and creativity to bring about change?	1	2	3	4	5	6	7	8	9	10

Appendix B

Eight Dimensions and Factor Loadings for Organizational Capacity for Change

Item #	Question	Factor loadings
	Do the unit leader(s)	**Factor 1: Trustworthy leaders**
01	protect the core values while encouraging change?	0.708
02	consistently articulate an inspiring vision of the future?	0.738
03	show courage in their support of change initiatives?	0.709
04	demonstrate humility while fiercely pursuing the vision?	0.718
	Do we have an organizational culture that	**Factor 2: Innovative culture**
05	values innovation and change?	0.509
06	attracts and retains creative people?	0.693
07	provides resources to experiment with new ideas?	0.726

Item #	Question	Factor loadings
08	allows people to take risks and occasionally fail?	0.691
	Does information flow effectively	**Factor 3: Communication systems**
09	from executives to workers?	0.745
10	in a timely fashion?	0.772
11	across organizational units?	0.787
12	from customers to the business unit?	0.734
	Do middle managers in this organizational unit	**Factor 4: Involved midmanagers**
13	effectively link top executives with frontline employees?	0.565
14	show commitment to the organization's well-being?	0.660
15	balance change initiatives while getting work done?	0.727
16	voice dissent constructively?	0.676
	Do frontline employees	**Factor 5: Trusting followers**
17	open themselves to consider change proposals?	0.773
18	have opportunities to voice their concerns about change?	0.609

Item #	Question	Factor loadings
19	generally know how change will help the business unit?	0.712
20	generally view top management as trustworthy?	0.535
	Do employees throughout the organizational unit	**Factor 6: Accountable culture**
21	experience consequences for outcomes of their actions?	0.697
22	meet deadlines and honor resource commitments?	0.717
23	accept responsibility for getting work done?	0.780
24	have clear roles for who has to do what?	0.668
	Do change champions recognize the	**Factor 7: Systems thinking**
25	interdependent systems implications of change?	0.676
26	importance of institutionalizing change?	0.790
27	need to realign incentives with desired changes?	0.806
28	value of addressing causes rather than symptoms?	0.639
	Do we have change	**Factor 8: Capable**

Item #	Question	Factor loadings
	champion(s) who	**champions**
29	command the respect of the members in the unit?	0.776
30	possess good interpersonal skills?	0.804
31	are willing and able to challenge the status quo?	0.797
32	have the will and creativity to bring about change?	0.667

Source: Judge and Douglas (2009), p. 648.

Appendix C:

Organizational Capacity for Change Benchmarking Descriptive Statistics

Table 14.1 Descriptive Statistics for Strategic Business Units

OCC dimension	Mean value	Standard deviation	Coefficient of variation
1. Trustworthy leadership	27.1	4.7	0.17
2. Trusting followers	24.7	4.3	0.17
3. Capable champions	26.1	4.9	0.19
4. Involved midmanagement	26.2	4.5	0.17
5. Systems thinking	25.9	4.1	0.21
6. Communications systems	23.4	4.8	0.21
7. Accountable culture	26.0	4.3	0.17
8. Innovative culture	24.6	4.6	0.19
Overall organization			
Aggregate scores:	204.0		

Source: These data represent the descriptive statistics on organizational capacity for change across the eight dimensions for

5,124 employees assessing their organizational capacity for change within 205 strategic business units for firms operating in North America, Europe, and Asia during 1999 to 2006. The coefficient of variation is the standard deviation divided by the mean value. The higher the coefficient of variation, the more variation or volatility is experienced with this particular organizational attribute.

Appendix D:

Organizational Capacity for Change Benchmarking Hierarchical Subgroups

Table 15.1 Mean Values for Hierarchical Subgroups within SBUs

OCC dimension	Senior executives	Midmanagers	Frontline workers
1. Trustworthy leadership	29.2	27.9	26.4
2. Trusting followers	25.6	25.0	24.7
3. Capable champions	27.8	26.7	26.0
4. Involved midmanagement	27.6	27.0	25.8
5. Systems thinking	27.1	26.2	25.6
6. Communications systems	25.8	24.2	22.6
7. Accountable culture	26.8	26.2	26.5
8. Innovative culture	27.0	26.0	25.0
Overall organization			
Aggregate scores:	216.8	209.2	202.6

Source: These data represent the descriptive statistics on organizational capacity for change across the eight dimensions for 5,124 employees assessing their organizational capacity for change within 205 strategic business units for firms operating in North America, Europe, and Asia during 1999 to 2006.

Appendix E:

Additional Resources

16.1 Simulations on Building Organizational Capacity and Leading Change

Judge, W., & Hill, L. (2010). Change management: Power and influence. Retrieved from http://hbr.org/product/change-management-harvard-managementor- online-modu/an/6789E-HTM-ENG?Ntt= change%2520management%2520power%2520and%2520influence

In this single-player simulation produced by Harvard Business Publishing in Boston, students play one of two roles at a sunglass manufacturing firm and face the challenges associated with implementing an organization-wide environmental sustainability initiative. The initiative seeks to change raw material inputs in order to make the company's products more "green" and also to address environmental waste issues. The simulation includes up to four scenarios with different combinations of two important factors for creating change: the relative power of the change agent and the relative urgency associated with the change initiative. In each scenario, students choose among different change levers in an attempt to persuade key members of the organization to adopt the change initiative. Students are assessed on their ability to achieve the greatest percentage of adopters within the company while simultaneously using the fewest resources. Appropriate for use in undergraduate, graduate, and executive business programs.

ExperiencePoint. (2010). Experience change simulations. Retrieved from http://www.experiencepoint.com/

In this single-player simulation produced by ExperiencePoint in Toronto, students play the role of a change agent in four different organizational contexts. For the *GlobalTech* simulation, players lead change in a siloed organization that needs to be more customer focused. For the *SkyTech* simulation, players lead a corporate social responsibility initiative in a global corporation. For the *Lakeview* simulation, players implement lean practices to reduce patient wait times in a hospital emergency department. For the *Central-Valley view* simulation, players balance the needs of internal and external stakeholders as they lead the merger of two hospitals.

16.2 Other Books and Articles on Aspects of Organizational Capacity for Change

- Beer, M., & Eisenstadt, R. (1994). Developing an organization capable of implementing strategy and learning. *Human Relations, 49,* 597–620.
- Bennett, J. L. (2000). *Leading the edge of change: Building individual and organizational capacity for the evolving nature of change.* Mooresville, NC: Paw Print Press.

- Bethune, G. (1998). *From worst to first: Behind the scenes of Continental's remarkable comeback.* New York, NY: Wiley.

- Bishop, C. (2000). *Making change happen one person at a time: Assessing change capacity within your organization.* New York, NY: AMACON.

- Collins, J., & Porras, J. (1994). *Built to last: Successful habits of visionary companies.* New York, NY: HarperBusiness.

- Dell, M. (2000). *Direct from Dell:* Strategies that revolutionized an industry. New York, NY: HarperBusiness.

- Fullan, M. (2008). *The six secrets of change: What the best leaders do to help their organizations survive and thrive.* San Francisco, CA: Jossey-Bass.

- Gardner, H. (2004). *Changing minds: The art and science of changing our own and other people's minds.* Boston, MA: Harvard Business School Press.

- Gerstner, L. (2002). *Who says elephants can't dance?* New York, NY: HarperBusiness.

- Hock, D. (2005). *One from many: VISA and the rise of chaordic organization.* San Francisco, CA: Berrett-Koehler.

- Judge, W., & Blocker, C. (2008). Organizational capacity for change and strategic ambidexterity: Flying the plane while rewiring it. *European Journal of Marketing, 42*(9/10), 915–926.

- Judge, W., & Douglas, T. (2009). The evolution of the organizational capacity for change construct. *Journal of Organizational Change Management, 22(6),* 635–649.

- Judge, W., & Elenkov, D. (2005). Organizational capacity for change and environmental performance: An empirical assessment of Bulgarian firms. *Journal of Business Research, 58,* 894–901.

- Judge, W., Naoumova, I., Douglas, T., & Kouzevol, N. (2009). Organizational capacity for change and firm performance in Russia. *International Journal of Human Resource Management, 20*(8), 1737–1752.

- Lawler, E., & Worley, C. (2006). *Built to change: How to achieve sustained organizational effectiveness.* San Francisco, CA: Jossey-Bass.

- Lengnick-Hall, C., & Beck, T. (2005). Adaptive fit versus robust transformation: How organizations respond to environmental change. *Journal of Management, 31*(5), 738–757.

- Price Waterhouse. (1996). *The paradox principles: How high performance companies manage chaos, complexity, and contradiction to achieve superior results.* Chicago, IL: Irwin.

- Seidman, D. (2007). *How: Why how we do anything means everything in business (and in life).* Hoboken, NJ: Wiley

- Staber, U., & Sydow, J. (2002). Organizational adaptive capacity: A structuration perspective. *Journal of Management Inquiry, 11*, 408–424.

- Thames, R., & Webster, D. (2009). *Chasing change: Building organizational capacity in a turbulent environment.* Hoboken, NJ: Wiley.

References

Abrahamson, E. (2000, July/August). Change without pain. *Harvard Business Review, 83*(4), 75–79.

Alvesson, M. (2002). *Understanding organizational culture.* Thousand Oaks, CA: Sage.

Anastasiou, S. (1998). Communicating change. *New Zealand Management, 45*(9), 86.

Anonymous. (2010). Information technology investments in the United States. Retrieved August 20, 2010, from http://www.brainmass.com/library/viewposting.php?posting_id=169315

Argyris, C. (1993). *Knowledge for action. A guide to overcoming barriers to organizational change.* San Francisco, CA: Jossey-Bass.

Armenakis, A., Harris, S., & Mossholder, K. (1993). Creating readiness for organizational change. *Human Relations, 46*(6), 681–703.

Arond-Thomas, M. (2009). Do you have CEO disease? *Physician Executive, 35*(2), 78–81.

Balogun, J., & Hailey, V. (2008). *Exploring strategic change (3rd ed.).* London, England: Prentice-Hall.

Balogun, J., & Johnson, G. (2004). Organizational restructuring and middle manager sensemaking. *Academy of Management Journal, 47,* 523–549.

Barnard, C. (1938). *The functions of the executive.* Cambridge, MA: Harvard University Press.

Barney, J. (1986). Organizational culture: Can it be a source of sustained competitive advantage? *Academy of Management Review, 11*(3), 656–666.

Barney, J., & Hansen, M. (1994). Trustworthiness as a source of competitive advantage. *Strategic Management Journal, 15,*175–190.

Basset-Jones, N. (2005). The paradox of diversity management, creativity and innovation. *Creativity and Innovation Management, 14*(2), 169–175.

Becera, M., & Gupta, A. (1999). Perceived trustworthiness within the organization: The moderating impact of communication frequency on trustor and trustee effects. *Organization Science, 14,* 32–44.

Beer, M., & Nohria, N. (Eds.). (2000). *Breaking the code of change.* Boston, MA: Harvard Business School Press.

Bellman, G. (2001). *Getting things done when you are not in charge (2nd ed.).* San Francisco, CA: Berrett-Koehler Press.

Bennett, J. (2000). *Leading the edge of change: Building individual and organizational capacity for the evolving nature of change.* Mooresville, NC: Paw Print Press.

Bennis, W. (1999a). The end of leadership: Exemplary leadership is impossible without full inclusion, initiatives, and cooperation of followers. *Organizational Dynamics, 28*(1), 71–80.

Bennis, W. (1999b). New leadership. *Executive Excellence, 16*(11), 7–8.

Bennis, W., & Nanus, B. (1997). *Leaders: Strategies for taking charge.* New York, NY: Harper & Row.

Bonini, S., Hintz, G., & Mendonca, L. (2008). Addressing consumer concerns about climate change. *McKinsey Quarterly, 2,* 52–60.

Booher, D. (2002). Crisis communication. *Executive Excellence, 19*(1), 6.

Bossidy, L., & Charan, R. (2002). *Execution: The discipline of getting things done.* New York, NY: Crown.

Bowen, D., & Ostroff, C. (2004). Understanding HRM–firm performance linkages: The role of the "strength" of the HRM system. *Academy of Management Review, 29*(2), 203–221.

Brafman, O., & Beckstrom, R. (2006). *The starfish and the spider: The unstoppable power of leaderless organizations.* New York, NY: Penguin.

Brownell, E. (2000). How to create organizational trust. *Manage, 52*(2), 10–11.

Buchen, I. (2005). Training future manager-leaders. *Performance Improvement, 44*(8), 20–23.

Bunker, B., & Alban, B. (1997). *Large group interventions: Engaging the whole system for rapid change.* San Francisco, CA: Jossey-Bass.

Burton, R., Lauridsen, J., & Obel, B. (2004). The impact of organizational climate and strategic fit on firm performance. *Human Resource Management, 43*(1), 67–87.

Cameron, K., & Quinn, R. (1999). *Diagnosing and changing organizational culture.* Reading, MA: Addison-Wesley.

Carpenter, M. (2009). *An executive's primer on the strategy of social networks.* New York, NY: Business Expert Press.

Case, J. (2005, March). The power of listening. *Inc. Magazine*, 76–85.

Chaleff, I. (2009). *The courageous follower: Standing up to and for our leaders.* San Francisco, CA: Berrett-Koehler.

Chandler, G., Keller, C., & Lyon, D. (2000). Unraveling the determinants and consequences of innovation-supportive organizational culture. *Entrepreneurship Theory and Practice, 25*(1), 59–77.

Chawla, A., & Kelloway, E. K. (2004). Predicting openness and commitment to change. *Leadership & Organizational Development Journal, 25*(5/6), 485–502.

Child, J., & Rodrigues, S. (2004). Repairing the breach of trust in corporate governance. *Corporate Governance: An International Review, 12*(2), 143–152.

Christensen, C. (1997). *The innovator's dilemma.* Boston, MA: Harvard Business School Press.

Cohen, A., & Bradford, D. (2005). *Influence without authority (2nd ed.).* Hoboken, NJ: Wiley.

Collins, J. (2001a, October). Good to great. *Fast Company,* 38–45.

Collins, J. (2001b). *Good to great: Why some companies make the leap…and others don't.* New York, NY: HarperBusiness.

Collins, J., & Porras, J. (1994). *Built to last: Successful habits of visionary companies.* New York, NY: HarperBusiness.

Cook, K. (2001). *Trust in society.* New York, NY: Russell Sage.

Covey, S. (1989). *The seven habits of highly effective people.* New York, NY: Free Press.

Currall, S., & Epstein, M. (2003). The fragility of organizational trust: Lessons from the rise and fall of Enron. *Organizational Dynamics, 32*(2), 193–213.

Das, T., & Teng, B. (2004). The risk-based view of trust: A conceptual framework. *Journal of Business and Psychology, 19*(1), 85–101.

Davenport, T. (2009, February). How to design smart business experiments. *Harvard Business Review, 87*(2), 69–76.

Davis, S. (1997). What's your emotional bandwidth? Forbes, 160(1): 233-234

DeLong, T., & Vijayaraghavan, V. (2003, June). Let's hear it for B players. *Harvard Business Review, 81*(6), 96–102.

Deming, W. (1986). *Out of the crisis.* Boston, MA: MIT Press.

Denning, S. (2007). *The secret language of leadership: How leaders inspire action through narrative.* San Francisco, CA: Jossey-Bass.

Deutschman, A. (2004, December). The fabric of creativity. *Fast Company,* 54–62.

Dittmar, J., Jennings, K., & Stahl-Wert, J. (2007). Trust and engagement. *Leadership Excellence, 24*(11), 8.

Drickhamer, D. (2004). Talking the walk. *Industry Week, 253*(9), 76.

Drucker, P. (1996). Innovation imperative. *Executive Excellence, 13*(12): 7–8.

Drucker, P. (1993). *Innovation and entrepreneurship.* New York, NY: HarperCollins.

Drucker, P. (1992, September/October). The new society of organizations. *Harvard Business Review, 70*(5), 95–105.

Duck, J. (2001). *The change monster: The human forces that fuel or foil corporate transformation and change.* New York, NY: Random House.

Dutton, J., Ashford, S., O'Neill, R., & Lawrence, K. (2001). Moves that matter: Issue selling and organizational change. *Academy of Management Journal, 44,*716–736.

Edmondson, A. (2002). The local and variegated nature of learning in organizations: A group-level perspective. *Organization Science, 13*(2): 128–146.

Edmondson, A. (2008, July/August). The competitive imperative of learning. *Harvard Business Review*, 86(7/8), 60–67.

Farmer, N. (2008). *The invisible organization: How informal networks can lead organizational change.* London, England: Ashgate.

Farson, R., & Keyes, R. (2002, August). The failure-tolerant leader. *Harvard Business Review*, 80(8), 64–71.

Fisher, R., & Sharp, A. (2004). *Lateral leadership: Getting things done when you are not in charge (2nd ed.).* New York, NY: Profile Books.

Fitzgerald, S., & Schutte, N. (2010). Increasing transformational leadership through enhancing self-efficacy. *Journal of Management Development, 29*(5), 495–515.

Florida, R. (2002). *The rise of the creative class.* New York, NY: Perseus Books.

Floyd, S., & Wooldridge, W. (1996). *The strategic middle manager: How to create and sustain competitive advantage.* San Francisco, CA: Jossey-Bass.

Garvin, D. (2004, July/August). What every CEO should know about new businesses. *Harvard Business Review*, 18–21.

Gerstner, L. (2002). *Who says elephants can't dance?* New York, NY: HarperBusiness.

Gharajedaghi, J. (2007). Systems thinking: A case for second-order learning. *Learning Organization, 14*(6), 473–479.

Gilbert, M. (2005). *The workplace revolution: Restoring trust in business and bringing meaning to our work.* York Beach, ME: Conari Press.

Gladwell, M. (2002). *The tipping point: How little things can make a big difference.* New York, NY: Little, Brown.

Goffee, R., & Jones, G. (2000, September/October). Why should anyone be led by you? *Harvard Business Review, 78*(5), 63–70.

Goffee, R., & Jones, G. (2006). *Why should anyone be led by you? What it takes to be an authentic leader.* Boston, MA: Harvard Business School Press.

Goldsmith, M. (2008). Just be you. *Leadership Excellence, 25*(11), 20.

Goldsmith, M., & Morgan, H. (2003). Leadership is a contact sport: The "follow-up factor" in management development. Retrieved on July 10, 2010 fromhttp://www.marshallgoldsmithlibrary.com/docs/articles/LeaderContactSport.pdf

Granovetter, M. (1973). *The strength of weak ties. American Journal of Sociology, 78*(6), 1360–1380.

Grey, C., & Garsten, C. (2001). Trust, control, and post-bureaucracy. *Organization Studies, 22*(2), 229–251.

Grove, A. (1996). *Only the paranoid survive*: How to exploit the crisis points that challenge every company and career. New York, NY: Doubleday.

Hall, D. (2007, June 25). Fail fast, fail cheap. *Business Week*, 32.

Hall, S. (2008). BPM change: How a company can prepare. *Business Performance Management, 6*(1), 19–24.

Hallier, J., & James, P. (1997). Middle managers and the employee psychological contract: Agency, protection and advancement. *Journal of Management Studies, 34*(5), 703–723.

Hallier, J., & Lyon, P. (1996). Job insecurity and employee commitment: Managers' reactions to the threat and outcomes of redundancy selection. *British Journal of Management, 7*(1), 107–124.

Hamel, G., & Prahalad, C. K. (1994). *Competing for the future.* Boston, MA: Harvard Business School Press.

Hammer, M. (2004, April). Deep change: How operational innovation can transform your company. *Harvard Business Review, 82*(4), 85–93.

Hammond, S., & Mayfield, A. (2004). *The thin book of naming elephants: How to surface undiscussables for greater organizational success.* Bend, OR: Thin Book.

Hampden-Turner, C. (1992). *Creating corporate culture.* Reading, MA: Addison-Wesley.

Hanna, D. (2010, March 8). How GM destroyed its Saturn success. *Forbes*, 28.

Hardy, B. (2007). Linking trust, change, leadership and innovation. *Knowledge Management Review, 10*(5), 18–24.

Hargadon, A., & Sutton, R. (2000, May/June). Building an innovation factory. *Harvard Business Review*, 157–166.

Harris, P. (2010). Leadership role models earn trust and profits. *Training and Development, 64*(3), 47–51.

Heath, D., & Heath, C. (2008, February). Make goals not resolutions. *Fast Company, 122,* 58–59.

Hebel, M. (2007). Light bulbs and change: Systems thinking and organizational learning for new ventures. *Learning Organization, 14*(6), 499–511.

Heneman, R., Fisher, M., & Dixon, K. (2001). Reward and organizational systems alignment: An expert system. *Compensation and Benefits Review, 33*(6), 18–30.

Henttonen, K., & Blomqvist, K. (2005). Managing distance in a global virtual team: The evolution of trust through technology-mediated relational communication. *Strategic Change, 14*(2), 107–119.

Higgins, J., & McAllaster, C. (2004). If you want strategic change, don't forget to change your cultural artifacts. *Journal of Change Management, 4*(1), 63–74.

Higgs, M., & Rowland, D. (2005). All changes great and small: Exploring approaches to change and its leadership. *Journal of Change Management, 5*(2), 121–151.

Hinduan, Z., Wilson-Evered, E., Moss, S., & Scanell, E. (2009). Leadership, work outcomes, and openness to change following an Indonesian bank merger. *Asian Pacific Journal of Human Resources, 47*(1), 59–75.

Hurley, R. (2006, September). The decision to trust. *Harvard Business Review, 84*(9), 55–63.

Huy, Q. (2001, September/October). In praise of middle managers. *Harvard Business Review,* 72–79.

Huy, Q. (2002). Emotional balancing of organizational continuity and radical change: The contribution of middle managers. *Administrative Science Quarterly, 47*(1), 31–51.

Jelinek, M., & Bean, A. (2010). New innovation architectures will shape R&D labs of the future. *Research Technology Management, 53*(2), 2–5.

Jones, C. (2001). *Organizational trust, learning and performance.* (Doctoral dissertation, George Washington University, 2001). Accession Order No. *AAT*3006928.

Judge, W. (1999). *The leader's shadow: Exploring and developing executive character.* Thousand Oaks, CA: Sage.

Judge, W., & Blocker, C. (2008). Organizational capacity for change and strategic ambidexterity: Flying the plane while rewiring it. *European Journal of Marketing, 42*(9/10), 915–926.

Judge, W., & Douglas, T. (2009). The evolution of the organizational capacity for change construct. *Journal of Organizational Change Management, 22*(6), 635–649.

Judge, W., & Elenkov, D. (2005). Organizational capacity for change and environmental performance: An empirical assessment of Bulgarian firms. *Journal of Business Research, 58*, 894–901.

Judge, W., Fryxell, G., & Dooley, R. (1997). The new task of R&D management: Creating goal-directed communities for innovation. *California Management Review, 39*(3), 72–85.

Judge, W., Naoumova, I., Douglas, T., & Koutzevol, N. (2009). Organizational capacity for change and firm performance in Russia. *International Journal of Human Resource Management, 20*(8), 1737–1752.

Kanter, R. (1983). *The change masters: Innovation and entrepreneurship in the American corporation.* New York, NY: Simon & Schuster.

Kanter, R. (2004, July/August). The middle manager as innovator. *Harvard Business Review, 84*(4), 150–161.

Kanter, R. (2006, November). Innovation traps. *Harvard Business Review, 86*(11), 72–83.

Kaplan, S. (2008). Are U.S. CEOs overpaid? *Academy of Management Perspectives, 22*(2), 5–20.

Katz, D., & Kahn, R. (1966). *The social psychology of organizations.* New York, NY: Wiley.

Katzenbach, J. (1996). From middle manager to real change leader. *Strategy and Leadership, 24*(4), 32–35.

Kelley, R. (1992). *The power of followership.* New York, NY: Doubleday.

Kelley, T., & Littman, J. 2005. *The ten faces of innovation: IDEO's strategies for defeating the devil's advocate and driving creativity throughout your organization.* New York, NY: Doubleday.

Kempner, M. (2009). Trust is dead. Long live trust. *Chief Executive, 240,* 23–25.

Kerr, J., & Slocum, J. (2005). Managing corporate culture through reward systems. *Academy of Management Executive, 19*(4), 130–150.

Kerr, S. (1975). On the folly of rewarding A while hoping for B. *Academy of Management Journal, 18,* 769–783.

Kilmann, R. (1989). *Managing beyond the quick fix.* San Francisco, CA: Jossey-Bass.

Kotter, J. (1995, March/April). Leading change: Why transformation efforts fail. *Harvard Business Review, 73*(2), 59–67.

Kotter, J. (1996). *Leading change.* Boston, MA: Harvard Business School Press.

Kotter, J., & Cohen, D. (2002). *The heart of change: Real-life stories of how people change their organizations.* Boston, MA: Harvard Business School Press.

Kotter, J., & Heskett, J. (1992). *Corporate culture and performance.* New York, NY: Free Press.

Kouzes, J. (2005). Leadership development is character development. *Leadership Excellence, 22*(2), 6–7.

Kouzes, J., & Posner, B. (2003). *The leadership challenge (3rd ed.).* San Francisco, CA: Jossey-Bass.

Krishnamurthy, B. (2008, December). Use downtime to enhance skills. *Harvard Business Review,* 86(12), 29–30.

Kuhl, S., Schnelle, T., & Tillmann, F.–J. (2005). Lateral leadership: An organizational approach to change. *Journal of Change Management, 5*(2), 177–190.

Kydd, A. (2000). Trust, reassurance, and cooperation. *International Organization, 54*(2), 325–358.

Larkin, T., & Larkin, S. (1994). *Communicating change: Winning employee support for new business goals.* New York, NY: McGraw-Hill.

Larkin, T., & Larkin, S. (1996, May/June). Reaching and changing frontline employees. *Harvard Business Review, 74*(3), 95–104.

Lawler, E., & Worley, C. (2006). *Built to change: How to achieve sustained organizational effectiveness.* San Francisco, CA: Jossey-Bass.

Littlefield, K. (2004). The profile of the twenty-first century leader: Redefining today's progressive entrepreneurs. *International Journal of Entrepreneurship, 8,* 23–55.

Maccoby, M. (2004, September). Why people follow the leader: The power of transference. *Harvard Business Review, 82*(9), 77–85.

Maitland, A. (2008, May 28). Straight-talking is the key to success. *Financial Times, 2.*

Mayer, R., Davis, J., & Schoorman, F. D. (1995). An integrative model of organizational trust. *Academy of Management Review, 20*(3), 709–734.

McCall, M., Lombardo, M., & Morrison, A. (1988). *Lessons of experience: How executives develop on the job.* New York, NY: Free Press.

McCann, L., Morris, J., & Hassard, J. (2008). Normalized intensity: The new labour process of middle management. *Journal of Management Studies, 45*(2), 343–363.

McLuhan, M. (1964). *Understanding media.* London, England: Routledge.

Melnyk, S., Hanson, J., & Calantone, R. (2010). Hitting the target…but missing the point: Resolving the paradox of strategic transition. *Long Range Planning, 43*(4), 555–575.

Mercer, J. (2010). In praise of dissent. *Ode Magazine, 8*(4), 54–61.

Miller, J. (1978). *Living systems.* New York, NY: McGraw-Hill.

Mishra, K. (2009). J. Walter Thompson: Building trust in troubled times. *Research in Marketing, 1*(2), 246–266.

Mumford, M. (2000). Managing creative people: Strategies and tactics for innovation. *Human Resource Management Review, 10*(3), 313–351.

Nancheria, A. (2009). Future leaders expected to wield soft power. *Training and Development, 63*(12), 16–18.

Nordblom, C. (2006). Involving middle managers in strategy at Volvo group. *Strategic Communication Management, 10*(2), 26–30.

Norman, S., Avolio, B., & Luthans, F. (2010). The impact of positivity and transparency on trust in leaders and their perceived effectiveness. *Leadership Quarterly, 21*(3), 350–370.

O'Reilly, C., & Pfeffer, J. (2000). *Hidden value: How great companies achieve extraordinary results with ordinary people.* Boston, MA: Harvard Business School Press.

Osborne, J. (1993). The supervisor's role in managing change. *Supervisory Management, 38*(3), 3.

Oshry, B. (1996). *Seeing systems.* San Francisco, CA: Berrett-Koehler.

O'Toole, J., & Bennis, W. (2009, June). What's needed next: A culture of candor. *Harvard Business Review, 87*(6), 54–61.

Ouchi, W. (1980). Markets, bureaucracies, and clans. *Administrative Science Quarterly, 25*(1), 129–141.

Ozag, D. (2001). *A mixed methodology study of the relationship between merger survivors' trust, hope, and organizational commitment.* (Doctoral dissertation, George Washington University, 2001). Accession Order No. *AAT*3029589.

Parker, G. (2002). *Cross–functional teams: Working with allies, enemies and other strangers.* San Francisco, CA: Jossey-Bass.

Pellet, J. (2009). Rebuilding trust in the CEO. *Chief Executive, 242,* 58–63.

Pelley, S. (2010, May 16). Escape from Deepwater Horizon. In 60 Minutes [Television news magazine]. New York, NY: CBS News. Retrieved on June 12, 2010 from<u>http://www.cbsnews.com/stories/2010/05/16/60minutes/main6490087.shtml?tag=mncol;lst;2</u>

Peters, J., & Waterman, R. (1982). *In search of excellence: Lessons from America's best-run companies.* New York, NY: Harper & Row.

Peters, T. (2006). *Innovate or die.* Enterprise Media [Videotape]. Retrieved on July 21, 2010 from<u>http://www.enterprisemedia.com/product/00245/innovate_die.html</u>

Peus, C., Frey, D., Gerhardt, M., Fischer, P., & Traut-Mattausch, E. (2009). Leading and managing change initiatives. *Management Revue, 20*(2), 158–176.

Pfeffer, J., & Sutton, R. (1999, May/June). The smart-talk trap. *Harvard Business Review, 77*(3), 134–142.

Pfeffer, J., & Sutton, R. (2000). *The knowing–doing gap: How smart companies turn knowledge into action.* Boston, MA: Harvard Business School Press.

Prior, D., Surroca, J., & Tribó, J. (2008). Are socially responsible managers really ethical? Exploring the relationship between earnings management and corporate social responsibility. *Corporate Governance: An International Review, 16*(3): 160–177.

ProQuest Research Library. (2010). Organization change. Retrieved from http://www.proquest.com.

Prosen, B. (2006). Five crippling habits: Are they attacking your organization from within? *SuperVision, 67*(12), 6–8.

Pucetaite, R., Lämsä, A., & Novelskaite, A. (2010). Building organizational trust in a low-trust societal context. *Baltic Journal of Management, 5*(2), 197–217.

Quinn, R. (1991). *Beyond rational management: Mastering the paradoxes and competing demands of high performance.* San Francisco, CA: Jossey-Bass.

Ramo, H. (2004). Moments of trust: Temporal and spatial factors of trust in organizations. *Journal of Managerial Psychology, 19*(8), 760–775.

Rogers, E. (1983). *Diffusion of innovations (5th ed.).* New York, NY: Free Press.

Roth, J. (2008). Review of the book *The speed of trust: the one thing that changes everything,* by Stephen Covey. *People & Strategy, 31*(1): 57.

Schein, E. (1985). *Organizational culture and leadership.* San Francisco, CA: Jossey-Bass.

Schriefer, A., & Sales, M. (2006). Creating strategic advantage with dynamic scenarios. *Strategy and Leadership, 34,* 31–42.

Schwartz, P. (1991). *The art of the long view.* New York, NY: Doubleday.

Senge, P. (1990). *The fifth discipline*. New York, NY: Doubleday.

Shames, A. (2009, April 1). Einstein called it "combinatorial play" [Blog entry]. Retrieved on June 21, 2010 from http://innovationonmymind.blogspot.com/2009/04/einstein-called-it-combinatorial-play.html

Shook, J. (2010). How to change a culture: Lessons from NUMMI. *Sloan Management Review, 51*(2), 63–68.

Shrivastava, P. (1985, Winter). Integrating strategy formulation with organizational culture. *Journal of Business Strategy, 5*(3), 103–111.

Spreitzer, G., & Quinn, R. (1996). Empowering middle managers to be transformational leaders. *Journal of Applied Behavioral Science, 32*(3), 237–263.

Stamato, L. (2008, July/August). Should business leaders apologize? Why, when, and how an apology matters. *Ivey Business Journal, 72(4)*, 1–8.

Stern, S. (2009, February 17). Resources are limited and HR must raise its game. *Financial Times*, 14.

Stewart, T. (1995). Planning a career in a world without managers. *Fortune, 131*(5): 72–76.

Stringer, R. (2000). How to manage radical innovation. Why aren't large companies more innovative? *California Management Review, 42*(4), 72–88.

Stybel, L., & Peabody, M. (2006). Beware the stealth mandate. *Sloan Management Review, 48*(3), 11–14.

Taylor, K. (1998). Corporate change: If communication isn't working, nothing else will. *Employment Relations Today, 25*(1), 69–76.

Thames, R., & Webster, D. (2009). *Chasing change: Building organizational capacity in a turbulent environment.* Hoboken, NJ: Wiley.

Thomas, S. (2010). Turning conflict management into a strategic advantage [Unpublished white paper]. Retrieved May 25, 2010 from http://www.cpp.com/pdfs/conflict_whitepaper.pdf

Tichy, N., & Cohen, E. (1997). *The leadership engine.* New York, NY: HarperBusiness.

Ulrich, D., Zenger, J., & Smallwood, N. (1999). *Results-based leadership.* Boston, MA: Harvard Business School Publishing.

Vaill, P. (1991). *Managing as a performing art: New ideas for a world of chaotic change.* San Francisco, CA: Jossey-Bass.

Vaill, P. (1996). *Learning as a way of being: Strategies for survival in a world of permanent white water.* San Francisco, CA: Jossey-Bass.

Vlachos, P., Theotokis, A., & Panagopoulos, N. (2008, November). *Sales-force reactions to corporate social responsibility: Attributions, outcomes and the mediating role of organizational trust* (SSRN Working Paper Series). Rochester, NY.

Weber, P., & Weber, J. (2001). Changes in employee perceptions during organizational change. *Leadership and Organization Development Journal, 22*(5/6), 291–301.

Welch, J., & Welch, S. (2006, November 13). Send the jerks packing. *Businessweek, 4009*, 136. Retrieved January 18, 2011, from http://www.businessweek.com/perm/content/06_46/b4009127.htm

Welch, J., with Welch, S. (2005). *Winning.* New York, NY: HarperBusiness.

Wheatley, M. (2006). *Leadership and the new science*. San Francisco, CA: Berrett-Koehler.

Williamson, H. (2008, May 22). Merkel ally backs curbs on executive salaries. *Financial Times*, 2.

Wines, W., & Hamilton, J. (2009). On changing organizational cultures by injecting new ideologies: The power of stories. *Journal of Business Ethics, 89*(3), 433–457.

Wormeli, R. (2009). *Metaphors and analogies: Power tools for teaching any subject*. Portland, ME: Stenhouse.

Wylie, I. (2001, October). Failure is glorious. *Fast Company, 51*, 35–38.

Yankelovich, D. (2007). Social contract. *Leadership Excellence, 24*(7), 9–11.

Zades, S. (2003, September). Creativity regained. *Inc. Magazine*, 60–68.

Ziegenfuss, J., & Bentley, J. (2000). Implementing cost control in health care: Strategies driven by an organizational systems approach. *Systemic Practice and Action Research, 13*(4), 453–474.